Uses his intelligence to improve the existing state of knowledge
*Harjit S. Sandhu MS, MSW, PhD - Criminologist*

A masterpiece in terms of its crucial objective, thorough, authoritative.
*Dr. Don Allen, Social Psychologist - Professor Emeritus; Oklahoma State University*

"It is astonishing, the amount of useful information you were able to reveal. The data you uncovered made the miscarriage of justice clear to anyone. My only regret is that I didn't know about your services earlier!"
*Dr. Joseph Cwikla, Endodontist - Florida Medical Examiner*

Deception Management has definitely given me the upper hand, especially when dealing with career criminals who know the game.
*Officer Derek Machens, St. Louis County Police Department*

Very helpful; I encourage everyone to seek your services.
*Jhesi Klumpp, Charge Investigator, Barnes-Jewish Hospital*

Learned a lot! The course and book are excellent resources and valuable additions to my tools as police officer and police chief.
*Corey Bringer, Police Chief Canton, Missouri*

Best book I have read on the subject matter. Great job making the subject matter easy to grasp. Contained more information on detecting deception than most.
*Jim McGuffey, Ace Security Consultants*

Isn't it bull that some professors teach classes like Dr. Camp's Deception Management? My bf took that class and I made a mistake & cheated on him. I was hoping to never tell him. He asked me to write down what I did that day for his class. Then he started finding all these errors and stuff and I finally confessed. He ruined my relationship. You should not teach those things! *Anonymous Online Social Page Comment*

# Exposing Lies

# Deception Management

When Knowing is Necessary

David A. Camp, Ph.D.

Copyright © 2011 David A. Camp

All rights reserved.

ISBN: 1463743084
ISBN 13: 9781463743086

# Dedication

To Deverie Rudd the most beautiful, creative, supportive and caring person I have ever known – who also happens to be a photographer extraordinaire as well as my wife, my love and my reason for believing there is good in the world. To my daughters Kendall and Kelsey Camp who are always in my thoughts and dreams for the joy they brought me. To Elliot Freeman, a great Martial Artist with a zest for life, a one man force of nature and my best friend. Finally, but not least, to Stacey Lannert, a beautiful woman whose fierce, positive attitude has proven to millions that you should never give into adversity–even when all seems lost.

# Contents

**Section 1: Foundations** — 1
    Chapter 1 Deception Basics — 5
    Chapter 2 Studying Deception — 13
    Chapter 3 Behavioral Guidebook — 17

**Section 2: Deception Identification** — 25
    Chapter 4 Unconscious Behaviors — 29
    Chapter 5 Subconscious Behaviors — 35
    Chapter 6 Conscious Behaviors — 59
    Chapter 7 Expression Analysis — 73
    Chapter 8 Discourse Analysis — 85
    Chapter 9 Comparative Analysis — 101

**Section 3: Obtaining Information** — 106
    Chapter 10 Interviewing — 107
    Chapter 11 Anti-Deception Interviewing — 113
    Chapter 12 Taking Notes — 125
    Chapter 13 Control — 135
    Chapter 14 Eliciting Honesty — 139
    Chapter 15 Responding To Deception — 151
    Chapter 16 Overcoming Resistance — 155
    Chapter 17 The Deception Management Difference — 165

**Referenced Materials** — 167

**Detailed Table of Contents** — 177

# Acknowledgements

This book is the result of the wisdom, advice and knowledge of many people. Dr. Paul Ekman, the world's foremost emotion researcher; Jackie Babcock, my sister and nursing instructor who provided information and feedback on physiology and a lot of personal advice; Dr. Edwin Strong, a man of incredible integrity and knowledge; Gary and Peggy Johnston, friends that know the true meaning of friendship, common sense and being true to yourself. Finally, my father, who has shown that success in life, is more than the things you have but the care you can give. There are many students, colleagues and friends I simply do not have space or time to include.

# Preface

The effort to understand identify and control deception is Deception Management. Throughout history, people have been seeking valid measures to use in identifying those who deceive. Only recently, has the scientific method, been applied in such a way that can seriously advance the ability to detect deception.

Since the 1940's machines have been used to measure stress, with the assumption that stress and deception are intimately related. Most of the valid findings have come about since 2000. Research over the last decade has produced knowledge leading to methods and approaches that are significantly better than chance.

This book is especially important because most published works in deception are based on techniques that have since been proven invalid. This applies to many of the more commercialized training companies, especially those specializing in interviewing and interrogation (a staple among law enforcement and governmental agencies such as Homeland Security).

With few exceptions, those who have received this outdated training still rely on it as they make decisions and how they interact with individuals that potentially have committed a crime. Although these programs do assist in catching many criminals, their poor validity causes many innocent people to be treated as if they were criminals because of the high error rates involved.

Work is still underway in seeking out the very best approaches and as new finding emerge, many of the old and often embedded beliefs must be cast off and replaced.

Using the newest verified information will improve the ability to identify deception, keep the innocent from suffering emotional traumas, and still allow those that need to know, who to hold accountable.

David A. Camp, PhD

# Section 1

## FOUNDATIONS

## Warning!

If you expose someone's deception, you damage that relationship! When people deceive, they believe their deception is private information and when it is unveiled, they feel their privacy has been violated. As a result, trust, respect and rapport are damaged. To maintain the relationship quality, it's best to learn to ignore the deceptions of others or at least, keep it to yourself. If you have a good reason to reveal the deception, keep in mind the damage that will result.

## What is Deception Management?

Deception Management is a comprehensive program for identifying various forms of interpersonal communications with deception identification and control being the central point. The contents making up Deception Management (DM) are the result of many human sciences. The efforts to identify 'Hidden Human Communications" include the areas of anthropology, criminology, body language (kinesiology), linguistics, psychology, psychiatry, psycho-physiology and sociology.

Merging the key characteristics of scientific and theoretically based deception information provides the core techniques that can significantly improve effectiveness. For the average person without training, increases in effectiveness of up to 63% have been demonstrated (a total accuracy rate of over 90%).

Numerous studies of the polygraph find that the machine is relatively poor in identifying deception. The polygraph is a machine of excellent reliability and validity as far as identifying stress, but that is all it does. Unfortunately, stress does not equal deception. The examiner must evaluate the reports of stress on the produced charts, compare them to the questions asked and decide the likelihood of whether a response was deceptive. Most deception training programs operate in the same manner. They seek to identify signs of stress and make a determination of whether the stress is the result of deception.

While many deception-related training programs exist, they generally share characteristics limiting their maximum effectiveness and can actually cause decreased success rates.

Several problems have been found in these approaches:

1. Focusing on a single technique or method of evaluation: This limits their maximum effectiveness to 70% (often less).
2. Deception Bias: From psychology we know that we tend to find what we are looking for. When looking at stress for signs of deception, we tend to have a bias and make the error of concluding deception where there was none.
3. Personal Subjective Bias: Contamination from a reliance on subjective beliefs and experiences. Since these are often the result of unrealized influences they are often invalid, yet they are presented and promoted as fact. When these unrealized influences are in fact responsible and are contrary to verified facts, those facts are often discounted further reducing the potential effectiveness of the trainees.
4. Unnecessary Training: They invest significant training time toward unusually unique or unlikely circumstances that are rarely encountered and what useful information they may contain is often lost due to lack of use.
5. Questionable Research Basis: Inclusion of research findings that were the result of biased and inappropriate investigation procedures.
6. Criminal Justice Focus: They are generally very focused on and designed for criminal justice applications which often further the spread of the misinformation due to the authority and prestige held by the law enforcement community.

7. Anecdotal Reliance: Because of the criminal justice emphasis, anecdotal experiences are often included as content filler. This is fine since people remember examples better than raw information, but if the experience related is not based on valid information this also continues the spread of misinformation.

"Educing Information", a report published by the National Defense Intelligence College, gives their evaluation on intelligence gathering techniques used in the US. The simply announce: "virtually none of them — or their underlying assumptions — are based on scientific research or have even been subjected to scientific or systematic inquiry or evaluation."

Such programs include several of the most common and popular interrogation and interviewing training programs. This is especially concerning since many spinoff programs retain these central themes and continue the cycle of misinformation that has existed for decades – if not centuries.

# 1 DECEPTION BASICS

## Introduction and Definitions

You do not have to fully understand how a car functions if you want to steer, accelerate or otherwise control it. However, you do need to understand deception if you wish to exercise control over it. Essentially, you cannot find or control something you cannot recognize.

In society there are many different and often conflicting definitions several include some of the terms used in this book.

To that end we must be consistent and precise when defining the various characteristics and components of deception. Most especially are these four very basic, very important and necessary terms: Deception, Lie, Truth and Honesty. So, for the purposes of this guide, we will rely on the following definitions:

1. **Behavior** refers to physical and mental processes and activities performed by people.
2. **Unconscious Behaviors** are reflexive behaviors or reactions that we perform but seemingly have little awareness of or control over. These include biological functions such as heart rate and sweating.
3. **Subconscious Behaviors** are similar to unconscious behaviors in that we are normally unaware of them. However, individuals can become aware of subconscious behaviors and with relative ease exert control over them.

Examples of subconscious behaviors include habits, speech patterns, behavioral mannerisms, body language, and so on.
4. **Conscious Behaviors** refers to the actions or behaviors that we are aware of and generally have complete control over.

Dictionaries define deception somewhat differently but are generally similar. Unfortunately we need consistency and precision rather than inconsistencies, vague references or contradictory explanations. For example, a web search quickly found the following definitions for deception: "misrepresentation", "misleading", "falsehood", "convincing others of untrue information" and "lying".

In common daily use, these are all fine. These all have useful elements. However, for identification and management purposes these seemingly similar definitions can completely mislead us. For instance, are misleading and falsehood actually the same thing? You can mislead a driver asking directions by pointing the wrong direction. But would that be termed a 'falsehood'? Is that lying? Is that "convincing"? In the same manner the term "Lie" is often defined in varying terms as well. Is a lie a deception? Must a lie be spoken? Can a lie be false information even if it is not misleading? As you can see, we must have carefully established definition if we want to become effective in identifying deception in its many forms.

Now that all that has been said, the following definitions will be used to provide the necessary precision and consistency for our use.

**Deception** is "knowingly leading others to false conclusions". Deception in human interaction is always a purposeful act. Unintentional misleading is either an accident or mistake or it may be what is referred to as deception by proxy (a concept we will address later).

A **lie** is "knowingly giving false or incorrect information"; In fact, a lie is often the exact opposite of the truth. For example saying 'yes' when you know the answer is 'no'. A lie is only one of several forms of deception. Lies often result when there is insufficient thinking time to create a different form of deception.

**Honesty** is a personality characteristic that includes the intent of trying to provide a response with the goal of leading others to correct and accurate conclusions. In short, honesty is opposite deception.

**Truth** is factually correct information. That said; you must realize that the 'truth' can be carefully filtered or edited so that it is purposefully presented to cause other to reach false conclusions. In fact, the most common of deception efforts make use of this approach. And it is often quite successful. Partly because we did not 'LIE' and partly if caught we can feel as though we committed a less sinful act because we did not tell an untruth. Truth based deceptions are more often argued as a simple misunderstanding rather than as an effort to purposefully mislead. For these reasons misleading (deceiving) by using "Edited Truth" is by far the preferred method of most people.

## Reasons for Deception

Given a choice, most people prefer to be honest and they tend to deceive when they believe they have a need to; when they have a reason. So, why do people deceive? While there are many possible motives for choosing to deceive, most are the result of thinking that if they are honest on such and such question; they might have to face some negative response: harm, punishment, loss, discovery of a secret, being viewed negatively, goal failure, and so on. These fears can be separated into two basic categories: Negative Consequences and Negative Results.

**Negative Consequences** are those things people prefer to avoid such as pain or punishment. **Negative Results** refers to a fear of not gaining something desired (such as employment, financial gain or even a date).

Although fear is the cause of most deception, some people deceive as a by-product of a mental disorder and others simply deceive for pleasure (controlling others, getting away with something, feeling superior, duping delight, etc.).

## Methods of Deception

Although there may seem to be an innumerable number of ways to deceive, actually there are only three principal methods: Content Editing, Question Avoidance and Redirection, and Response Falsification (lying).

# Content Editing

*Content Editing* is a form of deception that uses carefully selected bits of truth to encourage others to come to false conclusions. This method is used for several reasons:

1. If successful it avoids what might result from giving an honest answer.
2. It preserves your personal illusion of being an honest person since everything included was in fact truthful.
3. You can imply that any resulting 'false conclusions' were errors on the other person's part.
4. You can claim that you told the truth but simply forgot to include some details by accident.

The editing process: The deceiver evaluates the question posed, reviews and selects facts that will result in desired false conclusions and selects which facts to exclude that would likely lead to the questioner reaching the correct conclusion. Since the deception involves careful editing rather than mere information recall, this process is more mentally demanding.

Example: Little Johnnie was asked to go to the store down the street to get a loaf of bread. He was specifically instructed to go directly to the store and return home; He did go directly to the store as instructed but on the way home he stopped at the candy shop along the way. When he was asked what took him so long, he said, "I went straight to the store like you said". He simply edited (left) out the detour to the candy store and implied that he came straight home and has no idea why it took so long.

In order to identify this form of deception a careful evaluation of the response is necessary. Replying, "So you went straight to the store?" would get a "Yes" from little Johnnie; But if you notice he did not mention the return trip so asking "Did you come straight home?" would likely be met with a confession like, "Well I kind of stopped at the candy store."

# Question Avoidance and Redirection

The second most common form of deception is *Avoidance and Redirection*. In this approach the response appears to be an honest answer. However, the question, as asked, is never actually answered. To shift the focus from the details (which is how they avoid the actual question) the subject will often follow their near response with a redirection in the effort to change the focus of the interaction.

For example: Mom and 14 year old - John:

Mom: "John, what happened to the lamp?"

John: "Why? What happened?"

Mom: "It's broke. How did it get broken?"

John" "I can't say. Do you think the dog did it?"

Mom: "The dog is at the vet's, remember?"

John: "Oh yeah, that's right. Did the vet call to tell us when we can pick the dog up?

Mom: "No not yet, but I really want to know what happened to the lamp."

John: "Like I said I can't really say what happened. Anyway, I can help clean it up if you would like."

Mom: "No, that's alright John I'll do it."

John claimed he could not say. The reason he could not say is that if he did, he would get in trouble because he would have to say he did it. Second, John redirected the focus twice, once about the dog, and once about his willingness to help pick it up. In this situation a follow-up question of, "Why can't you say?" might have led to information that would have revealed the truth of the situation.

# Response Falsification

Response Falsification is another way of saying, 'outright lie'. It is giving a response that is contrary to the truth. Other forms of deception imply or infer a conclusion to maneuver others into assuming incorrect or false conclusions. Falsification (outright lying) specifically states the false conclusion.

Outright lies commonly occur when a person feels they must immediately respond to a question and are too anxious or otherwise mentally unprepared to try and edit the truth and any effort to avoid the question would be impractical, or otherwise undesirable. Another reason for a subject to lie is when confronted with a direct question that offers a limited response set such as in this example: "Are you over 21?"

While most deceptions involve a lengthier and more involved discourse, an outright lie often consists of a minimum of words. Whether the person limits their response due to anxiety, fear, shame, or some other reason, the result is the same – a very short, to the point and limited response. For example, if asked, "Did you do it?" suggests only one option: 'yes' or 'no'.

Several of the more accurate detection techniques prefer to elicit greater amounts of content through more involved interactions. This increases the opportunity to spot deception indicators. In order to avoid receiving minimal content responses, avoid direct questions that force immediate answers and limited response sets.

For example: If circumstances suggest a lie is likely, ask questions that allow latitude in how they may respond. Done properly, they will have the opportunity for editing which should discourage the outright lie in favor of avoidance or some other deception method that provides a greater chance of identifiable indicators to be clustered so that a reasonably valid conclusion may be reached.

For example, you believe an employee has been stealing from the cash register; the desire might be to confront them with a question like, "Did you take money from the cash register?" However, this demands an immediate answer and offers only two options of answer "Yes" or "No". Instead, ask, "The cash register has been coming up short for several days. What do you think is causing the shortage?" If they respond with "I don't know." a follow-up question such as "Well, I think it might be theft. Who do you think would want to do such a thing?" As long as the response provides little in the way of indicators, a continuation of the questions can continue. However, there are indicators to watch for that will and they will usually be present without extensive questioning.

# 2 STUDYING DECEPTION

The amount of research on deception identification is vast. Issues of crime and national security have made deception detection a high research priority. There are many problems with this type of research. A few examples illustrate some of these problems.

Possibly the greatest issue is trying to imitate the emotional motivations that underlie real life deceiving. Since most deception is emotionally caused, testing in a laboratory setting must try to duplicate the perception of risk and the experience of fear that would be found in real life circumstances. This is difficult because most methods of inducing fear would be considered unethical. This result is that lab research and field research reach different conclusions.

Another issue is that selection of methods employed in deception identification. Which methods should be use: emotion recognition, behavior profiling, discourse analysis, neurological imaging or what? Obviously, if this research were easy to accomplish there would be no need to resolve these concerns. As with most properly conducted research, deception identification achieves the best results when using multiple methods. In Deception Management many methods were evaluated for their strengths and weaknesses and a few of the most useable and effective methods were selected for use in concert with one another.

One particularly bothersome issue is that of self-esteem. This issue is a concern for a variety of reasons. One is especially serious with reference to deception training. Specifically, people believe they are good at lie detecting regardless of the fact that they are not. We are taught that being good at deception identification, is tied directly to our self-esteem. This is compounded by the discovery that the more someone believes they are a good lie detector, the worse they tend to score when tested. This is especially true for people in positions of authority.

Some exceptions do exist. One is the existence of 'naturals'. Naturals, also known as Lie Wizards, are people that achieve near 100% accuracy without being trained and often have no idea or awareness of how they arrive at their conclusions. In general it seems that about 3 people in a 1000 are naturals. Another exception would involve people that have been trained in one or more of the valid deception identification training programs.

Interestingly, two other groups stand out in their detection abilities: Secret Service agents seem to have an enhanced ability well above other federal agents and other law enforcement officers. Also professional poker players are above average in both detection and deception. It is possible these people are led to their career because they are undiscovered naturals, but no one knows for sure. Even these gifted professionals (not including the naturals) are rarely able to achieve above 70% accuracy. Still, 70% is still considerably above the 57% success rate of the general public.

With the Deception Management training approach, that is the merging of methods so that the weaknesses of one approach are covered with the strengths of other approaches, estimates based on research suggest that those so trained can achieve above a 90% success rate.

Evolution encourages success in deception. Because of our social and psychological upbringing our deception identification abilities are rarely better than guessing or flipping a coin. Why are we so bad at catching liars? There are four main reasons:
1. The Othello Error – Jumping to a conclusion of deception without eliminating other possible causes.
2. The Webster Error – Using vague, misleading and incorrect definitions to make conclusions about deception.

3. McDonaldized Lie Detecting – Making conclusions about deception based on a belief in the existence of a simple, perfect deception identifier.
4. Folklore Indicators – Relying on traditional and accepted indicators that are invalid but still remain widely accepted and socially shared - such as being shifty eyed.

With such bad scores overall, why do so many believe they are good at catching liars?

There are two main reasons:
1. If you don't catch a deception, you won't know you were deceived. So by not counting the failures, we evaluate our ability according to our successes.
2. We have to lie to ourselves about how good we are because we are mentally conditioned to believe the inability to tell liars from everyone else makes us a dupe or sucker, in other words we are failures. No one wants to fail.

Although we use incorrect definitions, have misguided beliefs that cause poor detection ability and don't notice the lies that work on us, we have been trained to never admit we may be wrong because then we would be socially incompetent chumps – not something anyone in the western world wants to be called.

# 3 BEHAVIORAL GUIDEBOOK

The knowledge and abilities involved in Deception Management stem from understanding the most relevant widely applicable rules of behavior. While there is only one behavioral principle described as a 'law' (universally applying to all people, no exceptions), the behavioral 'rules' apply to the majority of people regardless of culture, gender, or other human variations.

There are many approaches used in the effort to identify deception. All of them relate to behaviors associated with deception. The most common basis for deception is fear and there are several behavioral and physical indicators commonly associated with fear. However, in Deception Management other sources of indicators are considered as well. For example we look at abnormal behaviors, body/mind discrepancies, changes in how we interact, variations in our descriptions of things and a divergence between presented expressions and felt emotions.

When we deceive we also show physiological stress due to our concerns of being caught and labeled as a liar. The concern over being socially stigmatized with this label causes may of the same stress based indicators as seen with a fear of other more directly impacting consequences such as punishment, legal repercussions, loss and so on.

Deceivers that experience no stress (such as sociopaths and or those differently socialized) still present usable indicators; most notable are the changes in behavioral and communication characteristics.

# Why Deception Indicators Exist

Deceiving and deception are highly associated with several kinds of indicators, the cause of each stemming from different sources: While none are a 100% reliable, they are valid and when used together they provide confidence in determining deception identification. In brief deception:
1. Causes physiological stress.
2. Produces altered behaviors.
3. Requires more involved mental activities.
4. Is communicated differently than honest information.
5. Produces multi-channel conflicts not usually present.

# Rules of Behavior

The general rules of behavior apply to virtually all forms and types of behavior; including deception. While the rules apply to most situations and persons, the first rule is labeled as "The Law of Behavior" because it applies to all behavior and therefore serves as a basis for evaluating all human behavior. By learning the law and the rules as they apply to behavior interpretation we vastly improve our ability to differentiate between deception and other behaviors.

## Rule #1
### *Everything We Do, We Do for a Reason*

This behavioral law underlies everything a person does. Every decision, movement, word, thought, pause, stutter, or twitch has a reason. This means for instance, when a word or phrase is used, that word or phrase is selected over all other possibilities. For example, if a husband bought a new tool for $11.23 and his wife did not actually want him to buy any more tools at this time; he might announce to her that "It was only about $10.00." Instead of giving the actual amount he is trying to minimize her disapproval by minimizing the amount he claimed to have spent, without actually lying about it.

The importance of this law is extremely essential in any effort to apply Deception Management. Realizing the significance and learning to apply it in every circumstance is vital. For example, people often interrupt their speech with space fillers (uh, like, you know what I mean, well, so, etc.) to provide thinking time as they speak. This is not a conscious behavior, but a subconscious effort that serves a very specific purpose.

Similarly, when people don't do things they normally do, there is a reason for not doing them. For example, every time you finish a phone call with your significant other, you announce, "I love you" and this time you end the call with a mere, "talk with you later, bye." This is outside normal behavior and has some meaning.

## Rule #2

### *We Behave According to What We Imagine Others May Be Thinking.*

People constantly evaluate what others may be thinking about them and respond accordingly. Example: At a business meeting you take a break to get a drink from a water fountain. While doing so it malfunctions and squirts water directly on the front of your pants. You imagine that others will notice and incorrectly assume you "had an accident" in the bathroom. As a result you feel very embarrassed – regardless of the fact that no one noticed.

## Rule #3

### *Situations Thought Real, Are Real in Their Consequences*

Beliefs and actions have consequences regardless of their reality. In the previous example, your embarrassment impacted you so much you decided to not return to the meeting and miss some vital information that causes you to lose the negotiation.

Side Note: Another general guideline that can be quite useful and helpful is that people become less guarded when they believe they are smarter than you. Giving them reasons to think this can be a useful tactic.

# Rules of Deceptive Behavior

## Rule #1
### *People Prefer To Be Honest*

People will be honest unless they have a reason to deceive. In most cultures, except for specific social conventions and circumstances, honesty in interpersonal interactions is strongly encouraged as a basic rule of life. While there are exceptions, such as behaving abnormally 'appropriate' when meeting the parents of a date, responding to social greetings, surprise parties, etc., the general expectation of behavior is honesty.

## Rule #2
### *Clusters Are a Must*

Behavioral indicators MUST occur in clusters for accurate evaluations. Clusters are groups of identified indicators connected with a single question, concept or topic. Why? If you are observing someone and see one indicator associated with deception, you have a 50% chance of being wrong if you conclude they are being deceptive. With 2 indicators, you have a 25% chance of being wrong. With 5 clustered indicators you have about 10% chance of being wrong (a 90% chance of being correct in your assessment).

Example: At a nightclub, a young woman notices a young man across the room. Not wanting to seem too anxious to meet him, she makes very quick glances his way. On one such glance she sees him wink at her and she takes that as a sign of interest. However, the young man just has an ash or dust particle land in his one eye and he blinked that eye to clear it out just as the young woman looked his direction. Humans are very adept at recognizing when someone's eyes are contacting ours, so he momentarily locked eyes with her just as he blinked. His wink was actually a blink and her interpretation was incorrect. If he would have waved toward her when he winked as their eyes locked, her conclusion would have held more support (been more likely valid). <u>Note: The greater a subject feels the need to be believed, the greater number and strength of the deception related indicators.</u>

# Rule #3
## *How to Encourage a Lie*

The best way to obtain a lie, rather than an honest response or at least a truth based deception, is to put someone on the spot with a question they may have concerns about answering. Putting someone on the spot refers to a situation where you are requiring an immediate response to a question that is a sensitive issue or asking questions that an honest answer might cause embarrassment (not paying attention to behavioral rule #2).

# Rule #4
## *Prevention is the Best Policy*

It is better to inhibit deception than reveal it. Once a person has deceived, they have decided to not share the honest truth. This makes the hidden content their private information. Also since being caught in a deception has consequences, they tend to be very reluctant to recant their deception and honestly admit it.

# Rule #5
## *Baselines are Essential*

Behavioral Baselines are fundamental to behavioral analysis. Understanding the concept and its use is extremely important in determining behavioral significance.

## What is a Baseline?

In Deception Management, a baseline refers to a behavioral standard for comparison to future behaviors. In other words, if we can establish how a person behaves when they are being honest, we may be able to see a change in behavior when they are not being honest. Behavioral baselines consist of evaluating a person's physiological and psychological characteristics. Since, based on rule #1, we know that everything we do has a cause, we know that when a person's baseline changes, there is a cause. Although research shows some patterns occur more than others when people deceive, there are considerable variations from person to person. By combining knowledge of the general patterns with observations of baseline variations, we can begin to accumulate evidence of deception or honesty as we are evaluating a person's behavior.
Baseline Setting
In general, the goal of setting a baseline is to collect a behavioral standard for comparisons. Researchers and behavioral specialists typically set a baseline before the subject is presented with, or exposed to, information, questions, comments, etc. that might result in observable changes (whether they be emotional, physical or psychological). However, if a concerning or suspicion interaction occurs before a baseline can be set, an 'after the fact' baseline can be established if unexpected or necessary circumstances exist.

## How and What to Obtain in a Baseline

Commonly, a baseline is established (set) during causal interactions by observing behaviors and physiological reactions.

Deception Management training teaches a wide range of deception related indicators. There are two basic approaches to baseline setting. In the best case, we watch for the normal pattern of behavior associated with the most reliable and valid indicators of deception. However, if an interviewer (lie-detector) cannot become familiar with all those indicators, or they do not have the opportunity to observe those specific indicator behaviors, they should rely on those indicators they are most familiar with or the indicators that happen to be presented to them in a less controllable situation.

The two areas most useful are comparative stress and comparative deception identifiers. In comparative stress, the goal is to observe the subject in a set of low stress interactions. Initiate interaction about topics that have little stress inducing potential doing so in as non- threatening manner as possible given the existing circumstances.

Example: Use topics such as non-stressful demographics (where do you live, are you married, do you have kids, what kind of work do you do, etc.), friendly interest queries such as "how was the drive here?" or even questions about news or weather. Other topics can be irrelevant items such as "Have you ever gone deep sea fishing?" or "Did you see the game last night?" and so on. These types of questions allow the subject to interact in a manner that seems to be friendly, unrelated to the formalized interview and they are unlikely to generate deception. The goal is to identify how the indicators you will watch for are presented when there is minimal stress applied.

## What to watch for:

Observe areas most significantly associated with increased stress (speech tone, use of gestures, patterns of blinking, turning mentally inward to our internal dialogue, use of qualifiers, etc.)

In the 'deception identifier approach' the subject has already responded to a topic and the interviewer needs a lie for comparison. In this case ask them to lie.

For example, "I know you are a banker, I need you to tell me that you are a construction worker." This approach requires extreme care when observing minor facial and behavioral details. If you are proficient at emotion/expression recognition or differential behavior comparisons, this approach can be very useful.

The better you establish a baseline, the more accurate your conclusions are likely to be. As the various techniques of deception identification are revealed in the following instructions, the items most relevant for observation will be identified according to that particular technique. As you gain knowledge and are able to practice more techniques, your abilities will significantly improve.

Because minor and subtle behaviors are easily missed, using video recordings of the subject is recommended since these can be magnified, slowed down and repeatedly scrutinized.

## Habits and the Baseline

If possible, you should inhibit habits or behaviors that might serve as a distraction. These include behaviors such as smoking, eating, chewing (gum, tobacco or various objects such as earpieces on sunglasses), telephone interruptions, the presence of others, and so on. Such activities make valid observations more difficult.

However, if the situation is not under your control, you can make use of their habits by identifying their patterns when performing their habitual actions. This makes the habit part of the baseline and you can then recognizing changes in the habitual activities (style, intensity, frequency, etc.).

# If There's No Opportunity for Baseline Setting

What if you do not have the opportunity to set a baseline?

There are a variety of options you can try but only the last one mentioned below has any verified research to back it as reliability or validity. You can simply ask them to lie about something and see if they have any indicators that are obvious to the trained eye – but this likely takes extreme capability in using facial action coding. You can simple take note of what you know to be typical indicators and as you continue set the baseline as you go. The other is to simply avoid indicators of this type and rely on comparative behavioral signal disparities observed and follow-up accordingly.

# Section 2

## DECEPTION IDENTIFICATION

## Introduction

Knowing how to tell when a person is deceiving is an interesting hobby, but is it significant? In fact, deception can be extremely costly. According to Bureau of Labor Statistics (BLS), the average cost of hiring a salaried or professional employee is about $5000. They also report that almost half of those hired do not work out, necessitating a second hiring process and another $5000. This is especially relevant because most hiring failures are the result of decisions based on deceptive information.

Human resource studies found 33% of applications contain lies about experience, education, ability, and employment dates. One in ten use false credentials, fabricate experience, etc. to misrepresent their qualifications.

One often overlooked and costly error in the decision to hire a new employee is when an applicant has been hired and then let go, he or she can, and often do, challenge that decision in court. According to court records, over 60% of the ex-employees win the judgment. Paying $1000 for deception training can easily be recovered by avoiding even one deception based hiring error.

Another employment issue is that 63% of employees use sick time as personal leave time. While this may not seem to be much of an issue on the surface; it is a real concern because the actual cost averages $645 per employee per year. In other words, a company with 100 employees loses almost $41,000 per year on this relatively innocuous deception.

Yet another concern is that roughly half of all retail employees incorrectly charge customers. They give their 'friends' reduced prices, charge too much from others and pocket the difference or record the sale as if it were a less expensive item. Another 48% of retail losses are instances of employee theft. Altogether these issues account for 30% of business failures; most of which could have been avoided or greatly reduced if deception skills were utilized.

There are deception related problems beyond financial issues. For instance, it is well understood that medical personnel rely on obtaining quality information so that correct decisions can be made. A physician may make incorrect conclusions based on having flawed information due to a deceptive response. The diagnosis may be incorrect, the wrong medication prescribed, the wrong therapy applied and so on. Almost half (45%) of patients surveyed admitted to being deceptive with their physician. Such deception can result in errors that include unnecessary harm, malpractice lawsuits and damaged reputations to name a few.

While deception training can help in this situation, the interviewing component of Deception Management could be of more importance. Although research studies found that medical residents who received interview training demonstrated superior knowledge, attitude and skills when dealing with patients, interviewing techniques within Deception Management are specifically designed to enhance all aspects of interviewing while focusing specifically on techniques to obtain honest information. In other words, although interview training greatly improves a physician's interpersonal capabilities with patients, Deception Management interview training can further extend those positive outcomes.

What about in other professions? In some, deception is literally a life and death issue, not merely a money issue. In several notable cases, deceived social workers led to what would have been otherwise preventable deaths (most often of children or the elderly). This concern impacts issues such as child abuse, child neglect, domestic violence, elder abuse and abuses of the handicapped.

In law enforcement, police officers rarely get appropriate training of this type. However, detectives often do get some higher quality, though still flawed, training. Unfortunately the detective is not the 'foot soldier in the trenches' so to speak. The typical uniformed officer has the most contact with the public and is most likely to make important (even life and death) decisions, often on a daily basis; yet they receive the least training.

What about non-professional situations? Over 25% of marriages involve extramarital affairs which occur and often continue due to an inability to recognize basic deception indicators. Almost half (45%) of burglarized homes were victimized by someone who was able to deceptively gain the trust of the home owner enough to be given a house key.

Clearly these examples are the tip of the iceberg. Deception Management training is potentially the single most important, frequently usable and needed training available. Yet it is likely that most people will never consider such training.

Although there are five distinct approaches in deception identification each approach possesses its own strengths and weaknesses. A sixth approach is the coordinated integration of the five methods. This allows for three significant advantages: First, by using multiple methods in concert, the weaknesses of each individual method can be compensated for by the strengths of the other methods. Second, each approach can be used where it will be most effective. Third, when multiple approaches can be used together, they provide greater confidence in resulting conclusions. These advantages provide much higher levels of success than when approaches are applied independently.

While others are available, none are more reliable, with the possible exception of developing areas within neuro-imaging and the extraordinarily expensive and cumbersome equipment. Even with the use of MRIs, present capabilities are still not sufficiently sophisticated (and may never be).

The methods used in Deception Management are as follows:
1. Unconscious Reflex Behavior Analysis
2. Subconscious Response Behavior Analysis
3. Conscious Behavior Analysis
4. Expression/ Emotion Analysis
5. Discourse Analysis
6. Comparative Analysis

# 4 UNCONSCIOUS BEHAVIORS

For most situations, deception is the result of fear and activates the unconscious Autonomic Nervous System or ANS. The ANS responds to stress with biologically based reflexes including an increase in adrenaline production. The mental and physical stresses that result are unconscious and uncontrollable, thereby providing objective and distinctive indicators. Once activated, the ANS changes heart rates, respiration, heat production, muscle tension, pupil dilation, nervous energy and more.

One of the most commonly accepted beliefs in mainstream deception detection is that ANS activation can be a measure of deception. While there are limitations to this belief, it is scientifically supported that each component of the activated ANS system can be used to identify the presence of stress. If ANS activation is used in combination with other measures, it can be a powerful piece of evidence in determining potential deception.

Two major weaknesses exist with the ANS approach. First, identifiers must be recognized collectively (clusters) to reinforce that the signs noted are in fact stress related and not due to some other cause. Second, once identified as stress, deception is only one of the potential causes of its existence.

When using the ANS identification approach, the indicators identified in clusters must be also associated with a specific topic if the source of stress is to be validly identified.

# Cardiovascular

The Cardiovascular System (CVS) is comprised several components including the heart, lungs, arteries and blood vessels; all of which circulate nutrients, oxygen, waste products and other biological necessities or products throughout the body.

The primary functions most useful for identification are blood pressure, heart rate, blood vessel dilation and contraction, breathing rate and volume, heat regulation and sweating, energy availability, muscular readiness, pupillary reactions and digestive changes.

When stress is experienced, each of these produces variations that can be identified. For example, the skin of the neck and face can reflect changes in coloration (blotching and blanching) which often cause irritation in sensitive areas, especially those areas. The result is often an itching sensation, commonly identified by an urge to scratch or rub the nose.

With respect to the blood flow, when we feel fear, blood vessels in the upper body constrict (vasoconstriction) forcing blood to the lower body in order to provide the legs with the supplies necessary to support and enhance the ability to escape the situation at hand.

Alternately, in anger, the reverse is true. The blood is directed to the upper body to enhance fighting capabilities. As a result, the existence of felt stress can be identified and in some cases so can the emotion associated with the stress. A common identifier of anger is a reddening in the face, while a blanching or mottling of the face and neck suggests fear.

# Respiration

When the ANS system is activated, changes in heart rate and blood pressure demand additional oxygen so breathing increases to compensate.

# Increased Heat and Perspiration

The extra work performed by the circulatory system increases the body's temperature, ultimately increasing the need to rid the body of excess heat. Perspiration is the body's natural process for this purpose. Indicators of increased perspiration include sweaty palms, underarm perspiration and sweat on the brow. Because these are noticeable and often stigmatized bodily functions, the subject tends to make repeated efforts to disguise, hide or remove (wipe off) the perspiration – often in a surreptitious manner.

# Pupil Dilation

When the ANS system is activated, whether fear or anger, the pupils tend to dilate so that the eyes can take in more light (a basic survival response). This is considered by many researchers to be the single best indicator of an activated ANS system. Just as pupil dilation occurs with stress, studies show that pupil size also increases with increased mental workloads. Since deception is always a purposeful action, deceiving requires greater mental effort than honesty because a deception must be mentally prepared. As a result, pupil dilation is also an excellent measure of intensive thinking.

Further, research shows that the pupil dilates when emotions in general are aroused and do so virtually instantly, but the action slows as we age. Due to these factors, all of which are associated with indications of deception, many researchers consider pupil dilation to be the single best overall indicator among the stress based ANS reflex indicators.

Unfortunately pupil dilation is difficult to assess in real time due to lighting, eye color, level of eye contact, distance from subject and other variables. In situations where the opportunity is available, it can be one of the best reflexive stress indicators.

# Blinking Activities

There is a great deal of confusion, myth and misinformation concerning the role of eye blinking behaviors and deception. Part of the problem, even among researchers, was that research practices did not clearly identify what they are measuring, until recently.

Dr. Paul Ekman and others found that when we concentrate, our blinking rate diminishes significantly. In terms of deception, this means that while considering whether to deceive or not and while creating a deception in our mind, our rate of blinking goes down. This led to conclusions that any other blinking behaviors are probably unrelated to deceiving. However, Dr. Aldert Vrij examined blinking patterns of before during and after deceiving and found that as Ekman indicated, during the deception process we do slow down, but following the deception our blinking tends to suddenly increase. Alternately, non-deceptive respondents maintain a consistent pattern of blinking. We must be careful in evaluating this behavior and not jump to a conclusion of deception (Othello error). The concern stems from the fact that we tend to slow our blinking anytime we concentrate intently. We must make sure the slowed blinking rate is due to deception and not just careful consideration.

There are several considerations in making this determination:
1. Rate Changes: We must make sure the blink rate is a variation from the established baseline.
2. The Question: If we ask a question that requires deeper consideration, we should expect the blink rate to slow down. If a question that shouldn't require deep consideration is presented, we should consider a slowed blink rate as a sign of possible deception formation.
3. The blink rate of those deceiving tends to change from normal, to slower (during the creation and presentation of the deception) followed by an increase that exceeds the baseline.

In summary, in baseline setting we identify the subject's blinking patterns. When they are asked a question, a pattern change may indicate deception if it fits the above criteria.

# Muscle Tension

Muscle Tension refers to the increased tension or tightness of the skeletal muscles. As stress causes these muscles to tighten throughout the body, the subject will retain less control over the voice. The best indicator of this is the 'cracking voice' (at especially stressful points). Studies show that increases in voice pitch are the only voice pitch change directly associated with deception. But this is still only one indicator.

Other related indicators of increased muscle tension include 'jerky' limb movements (gestures that seem unnatural or awkward). This 'jerky' quality also occurs when we seek to exert conscious control over our general bodily movement. Such movement is an effort to 'act naturally' which serves to indicate they are trying to deceive about their stress.

# Nervous Energy

Although the increase of available energy is unconscious, how we seek to manage that extra energy is under our conscious control (covered more fully in Conscious Kinesic Analysis).

# Digestion

As the ANS system diverts blood and resources for fight or flight preparations, the need for active digestion is reduced and as a result, digestion slows. This is identifiable by stomach grumbling and similar noises.

Unfortunately, this is one of the least effective indicators, but it can still be used to support the validity of other indicators as a member of a cluster.

# Saliva Production

Stress causes a reduction or overproducing of saliva. If saliva increases, the subject tends to perform a noticeable 'gulp' to rid the mouth of excess saliva or if the change is a reduction of saliva, the subject's mouth dries adding the need to moisten the mouth and lips.

This is identifiable by the smacking sound of their lips sticking together and the subject's efforts to moisten them through licking, wiping as well as taking more frequent drinks, Again for these indicators to be meaningful they must occur in connection with other indicators and in a timely manner such as in reference to a topic of concern. If these changes occur in relation to an unexpected event or circumstance it indicates increased concern with whatever situation is being presented at that time.

# Summary

Because unconscious actions are generally beyond our control, they are very reliable as indicators of stress. It is very important to realize that stress has many sources and deception is only one of those sources. Jumping to the conclusion that indicators of stress must mean deception is present will significantly reduce success rates. Stress must be used as an indicator only. It is a very important indicator, but due to the many possible sources of stress, unconscious indicators of stress must be supported with clusters of additional indicators before a valid conclusion of deception can be determined.

# 5 SUBCONSCIOUS BEHAVIORS

Although the responses of the Autonomic Nervous System are reflex actions rarely available for conscious control, our subconscious behaviors are conditioned (learned) behavioral responses that exist just below our conscious awareness. However, they can easily be brought to the forefront of our consciousness. Subconscious behavioral changes such as habits and mannerisms include Expressive, Verbal, Vocal, and Kinesic (Physical) indicators of our body and mental processes.

Once a person realizes the need to control these responses, they are often able to exert a significant amount of control over them. However, because we operate many of these subconscious behaviors on autopilot most of the time, their automatic functioning produces a consistency and smoothness of action. When we must take conscious control over them, the required coordination is too complex and coordinated seamless conscious control is not usually observed.

For example, we make many errors when we first learn to drive a car. Accidents among new drivers are so common that insurance companies base much of their rates on the age of the driver. Why? Steering the car is the easy part. Keeping up with all the other aspects of driving (such as watching the other lanes, reading the road signs, watching the speed, etc.) greatly distracts from the simple act of steering. As people gain experience, our subconscious is teaching our bodies and mental processes to place many driving behaviors on semi-automatic. We learn to become highly aware when certain events occur (like seeing a police officer). Otherwise our driving is a mixture of conscious and subconscious action. The same is true for most activities that require multiple behaviors such as athletics, learning a musical instrument or acting 'normal' when we lie.

When people choose to take conscious control over these subconscious behaviors our poor multitasking ability means we can effectively manage only one or a very few conscious actions at a time. More than that leave us appearing poorly coordinated and produces unnatural appearing behaviors. This can be a significant advantage for the deception investigator because we know that being aware of these subconscious behaviors encourages us to consciously take control when we fear our actions may betray us (such as when we are being deceptive).

## Kinesics and Body Language

**Kinesics**, often referred to as body language, is the study of the meanings our movement and positioning communicate as we interact with others. Although the communicated messages are less precise than when using spoken language, kinesic messages are more honest in what they convey.

In general, people are unaccustomed to controlling every action and movement and the effort to do so is often referred to as 'Impression Management'. The ability to manage the impressions we present to others is the difference between good and great actors. A great actor dedicates their life to making this symphony of behaviors seem 'natural'. Most of us have not honed this ability and because there are so many components in 'acting normal' our efforts to do so seem more like a poor actor in a play - obvious and lacking a natural sense of coordination among the various parts that are necessary to be convincing; In other words, jerky and unnatural.

## How Body Language Indicates Deception

As previous discussed, when we feel stress our bodies reveal it. Even when we are aware of the stress responses, controlling the reflexive ANS is extremely difficult. Similarly, while achieving manual control of kinesic actions is rather easy, controlling them in a manner that appears natural is much more difficult.

Our kinesic actions are the result of a life-long training program where our body language becomes second nature through processes such as muscle memory. We can control these actions, but when we try to make our movements behave in a manner inconsistent our emotions, we have a conflict. This contradiction becomes magnified because our body language is normally under subconscious control.

Consider the example of something as simple as eating with silverware. We easily pick up the correct instrument, hold it correctly, and then use it to collect our food and deposit it into our mouth. We do this so well that a minor error such as food falling off a spoon into our lap is considered a social faux-pas. However, if you have ever injured your dominant hand and had to eat with the other hand you suddenly find that the muscles of that hand do not have the muscle memory of those tiny actions that help navigate eating without error. Although you can manage conscious control, your efforts appear jerky, uncoordinated and obvious. In other words, we can fake our kinesics, but without extreme amounts of practice they will not appear natural.

Imagine someone has unexpectedly thrown an object at your head. Your body through years of practice protecting your head from injury you smoothly perform a variety of coordinated actions to remain unharmed. You see the danger and in an immediate response you make several movements to evade being hit; your head moves sideways (seemingly without thought) while your torso and legs try to move your body away from the danger (usually backward). At the same time you know (unconsciously) that danger exists and you squint to protect your eyes while also raising your hands in a defensive action.

This complexity of motion is rarely realized. Trying to consciously fabricate and perform actions that are appropriate to a desired but false message AND do so convincingly requires significant skill that is available only through practice (if it can be fully achieved at all).

When a deceptive person is aware their body language may betray them, they often try to 'act naturally'. That is, they try to consciously determine how to act as well as how to present the act so that it comes across as convincingly smooth and coordinated.

This preparation requires time to mentally compute causing a response delay. Although this delay may be identifiable by itself, a more valid conclusion can be reached by observing the entire kinesic set of behaviors. Since they should be presented in a coordinated manner, but doing so is quite difficult without significant practice, you can watch for multiple indicators (clusters) that result from the difficulty they face in trying to coordinate these many precise actions and do so in a way that appears 'normal',

There are many observable indicators. Some of the more observable are efforts to inhibit the range of one's movements; for instance trying to control the size and speed of gestures in an effort to draw less attention.

An alternate indicator is the attempt to inhibit all body movement so that any potential 'kinesic leaks' that might occur are completely subdued. They do this by remaining almost motionless and generally appear to be frozen in their posture. For instance they may, cross their arms, put their hands in their pockets or simply sit on them. They may tuck their feet underneath them (if sitting) or cross their legs and hold them motionless.

While the indicators mentioned are very useful, the single best indicator is the lack of synchronization between their conscious efforts and their other forms of communication. Watch for discrepancies between body language, verbal content, expressions, and environmental conditions. As previously noted, when a message differs between verbal and other forms of expression, the non-verbal messages of the body are more honest.*

> \* **Important Note**: You will often hear 'body language experts' claim that a study by Dr. Mehrabian revealed that our words communicate only 7% of one's true meaning while tone accounts for 38% and kinesics 55%. However, if you hear this claim, beware! Dr. Mehrabian has been pleading with this community of 'experts' to correctly use his findings. Here is what he said was his findings: When verbal communications are ambiguous, the words communicate 7% of one's true meaning while tone accounts for 38% and kinesics 55%. In other words, when our words communicate clearly, they convey the majority of our communicated meaning. It is only when our words do not communicate clearly that our body language conveys the majority of the intended meaning.

Regardless of one's efforts to consciously control their body language, information almost always slips or leaks out. These 'kinesic leaks' are virtually impossible to completely manage.

It is important to realize that our emotions consume our conscious awareness, especially on highly emotional topics. The stronger and greater the number of emotions invoked, the greater the potential leaks that will occur.

Another use of kinesics is when someone changes their body language when a new topic is introduced or when a concerning question is asked. When this type of variation occurs and it is associated with a specific topic or question, no conclusion should be made until it is determined whether the behavioral change was a reaction to the topic or if it was merely coincidental. This can be accomplished by watching for clusters of indicators occurring at the same time and verification can be achieved by a repeat of the reactions if the topic is re-introduced at a later time.

Even when there is a reaction to the topic, we still must determine why the reaction occurred. **It is extremely important to understand that there are causes for stress reactions other than deception.** This is the primary weakness of the polygraph and other pure stress related approaches. Even with significant clustering of stress signals, this approach verifies the presence of stress but deception remains as only one possibility.

Example: a social worker is interviewing a parent about the bruises on her child. When asked if the husband caused the bruises. The subject reacts with a cluster of typical stress shifts and kinesic indicators followed by her verbally stating, "No, he didn't do it!" It would be easy to conclude she was lying, but the reality was that the mother caused the bruises and the husband had threatened to report her, but she had pleaded with him to not say anything. When the social worker mentioned the husband, the wife felt stressed due to a fear that he may be asked the same question about her and her fears of how he might respond were the cause of her actions.

**Deception is only ONE of the possible reasons for stress!**

# Summary

Stress can be identified through kinesic action. However, while deception often causes stress, the presence of stress means the person is feeling stress. It does not mean deception. If the stress is topically associated, there is a likely connection between the topic and the display of stress. If there are clusters, the topic is quite stressful but still not sufficient to conclude deception. To validate the existence of deception, the stress must be supported with external fact or other deception indicators that are not stress based.

# Actions Involving the Entire Body

The actions of the human body can be classified within a few types. Generally these include actions involving the entire body such as body positioning and posture, or parts of the body such as the face and eyes, non-gesture limb hands and feet use and the 'meaningful gestures' humans use such as the peace sign or the "OK" sign.

## Body Positioning

A **body position** refers to a person's stance, position or posture when sitting or standing. This mostly concerns which direction the trunk of the body faces in relation to others present as well as any environmental conditions that might influence the position taken such as windows, doors, furniture etc.

For example, we may squarely face the other party or stand or sit slightly turned away (such as a 45 degree or diagonal stance) or the "defensive" posture where the person is at a right angle to our stance, even though our faces are turned toward one another. Getting more precise information from this area of study requires considerable and extensive study.

People change body positions as a regular course of habit. However, when those changes are associated with a particular topic, they indicate stress and possible deception when discussing that topic. Of special significance is when someone turns their body away from an interviewer in sync with the introduction of a specific topic. This is a defensive posture that suggests stress. Movement into that posture suggests stress on the topic being considered at that time. To verify the stressful effect of the topic, bring the topic up again and watch for stress when it is re-introduced.

## Posture and Body Mirroring

Mirroring is the concept of adopting the same posture and movement style of someone else. We tend to mirror people we feel positive toward. This applies if we like them, have good feelings about what they are communicating or as a way to show our agreement with them. We tend to reject the mirroring of people we feel negative toward, do not like or are not in agreement with. Using this approach we can evaluate the meaning when there is a change of posture. The change reflects a reaction to emotions felt in the situation.

People withdraw from things they don't like. They back away when afraid, turn away when feeling shame and move toward things desired or liked. However, in very aggressive situations, movement may occur toward the things disliked as a show of defensiveness and a willingness to be aggressive. Other indicators (facial expression, voice tone, word selection, and physical stimulation) provide a clear understanding of whether movements are defensive/aggressive or friendly and agreeable.

## Other Full Body Movement

Body movements often reflect the fight or flight response. Specifically, we tend to move toward a subject of interest or someone we feel anger toward and we move away from things or people that we fear or feel disgust about.

# Face

Humans are highly attuned to faces. We pay a great deal of attention to facial movements and expressions. Because of this, we try to obtain control over our facial expressions; more so than any communication signal other than our efforts to control our choice of words. Because of the massive attention humans give to the face, many deception identification programs suggest that we should ignore the face because we tend to our facial expressions more than any other body language based communication making it the most unlikely to contain communication leaks.

This would be true except for the expressional research and training of Dr. Paul Ekman and others. These projects found that our face is a usable tool for identifying emotions regardless of the effort to keep those emotions disguised. While more research is needed, it is generally agreed that with training, our face does give away information we don't realize and even if we did, there is little we can do about it (see Expression Analysis).

The one approach that is somewhat usable within the ANS influenced approaches is the fact that the face is highly sensitive and when the ANS is activated, the more sensitive areas of the body (especially the face) react; often with coloration changes, a sense of irritation, and itching.

When feel fear, blood is drawn away from out face causing lack of blood causes the face and neck to appear mottled or blanched and along with the nose, this causes irritation or itching in those areas. The stressed person will often try to gain relief by scratching, rubbing or otherwise making contact with the irritated area.

Since this often occurs in interviews and social settings, the relief effort is often performed as inconspicuously as possible. As a result you can watch for "drive by" contacts or low key efforts to address the irritation while making it seem as though they are actually performing some other action i.e. removing glasses, brushing the hair, rubbing their chin, etc. If observed, pay close attention to the topic that immediately preceded the irritation-relieving activity. It is likely related to the cause of the stress.

## Yawning

Although there is a great deal of debate about why people yawn, only a few facts are available:

If we see, read, hear or otherwise indirectly experience a yawn we will usually have a (sometimes overwhelming) desire to also yawn. Some people yawn as a sign of tiredness. Some people yawn as a stall tactic to gain additional thinking time (such as when we need time to construct a deceptive response). When a person is honest, they rarely need additional thinking time to recall the answer to simple questions, and if they do need the time, they do not need to be surreptitious about obtaining the time.

However, people do yawn. So if we are going to consider a yawn as a potential deception indicator, we must evaluate it on evidence of the situation: Did the person's baseline include evidence of tiredness or yawning; Is there any external stimulus to yawn (such as someone else yawning). Does the yawn occur when a response is expected? Many people tend to yawn after smoking a cigarette or taking certain drugs. But these are usually fairly easy to connect.

Nonetheless, while yawning is not a strong indicator, it can be part of an overall cluster which should be added in if such a cluster seems to be emerging.

## Eye Activity

Eye movement can provide a lot of information about a person. Gaze aversion rarely indicates deception. Due to the widespread myth that a liar will not look a person in the eye many people will make sure to avoid that situation.

Others have gaze aversion as a normal baseline behavior – such as some cultures believe it in bad taste to look at someone in the eye for more than a brief moment as it indicate disrespect or even aggression. For instance traditional Japanese females were taught that this is a show of respect. However, that behavior would be noticed during the baseline collection process.

Still, gaze aversion may be useful if approached properly. When we feel certain emotions (such as disgust, sadness, shame, or guilt) we tend to look down and /or away.

If gaze aversion is not a baseline behavior and occurs in association with a specific topic, it may be considered as an indicator to group with emerging clusters. Similarly, any observed change in the manner of eye contact that occurs in conjunction with a topic and in coordination indicates a significant meaning which must be interpreted in accordance to the topic at hand.

The **Quick Glance** is a rapid head and eye behavior to watch for. The quick glance often follows a subject's response to a question of concerning content.

The quick glance occurs this way: The subject makes eye contact as they give their response. Immediately after they end their response they look down and away and then take a very brief (less than 1 second) upward glance to see if you bought into their statement.

While this often follows a deception, other reasons for the quick glance may exist. They may desire to avoid eye contact due to feelings of shame, fear, disgust or some similar emotion for reasons we are unaware of.

Regardless, the quick glance is worthy of notice and evaluation in light of the existing situation.

## Blinking

Determine a baseline for the style and frequency the subject blinks their eyes. When variations occur it indicates a change in their mental activities.

When the rate increases, it indicates emotional arousal and when it significantly reduces it suggests intense concentration or they are turning their attention inward (accessing their internal dialogue) to deal with a challenging issue such as coming up with a response to a question they may not want to be honest about. In general, watch for sudden or dramatic changes. Studies do indicate that consistency of eye blinking rates are associated with honesty and among the dishonest the rate begins at the baseline rate, then slows and then significantly increases finally returning to normal.

Another eye behavior of concern is also the center of a great deal of debate. This eye activity, called Lateral Eye Movements (LEMs) is also known as Eye Accessing Cues. The foundation of which is Neurolinguistic Programming (NLP) – a combination of physiology, neurology, psychology and linguistics). LEMs are thought to be useful in identifying specific mental activities that are identified by the direction a person directs their eyes when accessing information in their brains.

NLP suggests that a person looking left is generally remembering information while one looking right is accessing their creative abilities. While NLP advocates never claim these are related to lie detecting, many have concluded that it can be used as such. The claim is that a lie is a fabrication and can be identified by a person looking the wrong way when answering a question that should require recall not creative development.

Unfortunately, the lack of scientific evidence supporting NLP and these claims discourages using this approach. However, in Deception Management its application may be useful as follows:

When people are thinking, they often access their internal dialog and stare off generally in an unfocused gaze.

There is a distinct possibility that each person uses their eyes in a consistent manner for themselves, regardless of whether the larger generalization is valid or not.

While this has not been fully evaluated, if you choose to include it as a possible cluster component, then during baseline setting ask questions that are unimportant and seemingly irrelevant. The type of question will cause them to either create or recall information. As they do, take note of their LEMs. Re-establish this pattern with a few additional but non-sensitive questions.

If the subject is consistent in their LEM mannerism, those patterns can be included as part of the baselines established. This can serve to provide additional support for responses where additional indicators are needed to identify a concerning cluster. If a question requesting some form of recall is being answered with LEM actions that indicate fabrication the response may be further supported as potentially deceptive. If supported with additional indicators, the strength of a conclusion of deceit is increased.

How can you establish this? What kinds of questions should be asked? While the following are simply examples to illustrate the general approach, each situation may call for unique types of questions that can only be determined in the given situation.
1. What is the color of your car interior?
2. What will you look like in 10 years?
3. What is your favorite song
4. What would your favorite song sound like if slowed down 50%?

Generally the idea is to cause them to think about something they have not experienced and can only imagine as compared to memories that require a bit of effort. LEMs are generally useless for questions that are too easily available to the immediate memory such as, "Are you married?"

As research continues, this area of application may or may not receive support. If it does it may provide many additional possibilities of effectively reading how people are thinking.

# Limbs Hands and Feet

## Non Gesture Actions

Hand and arm movements are known as gestures that are grouped by their use. Most are classified as illustrators, manipulators or emblems. Some actions may serve additional functions such as when during stress as in a conflict situation, we pull our elbows close to the torso for protection by minimizing one's size, conserving heat and energy as well as reducing the limb's exposure to risk of injury. When relaxed, the arms either hang comfortably or are used expressively providing communicative gestures.

The common action of covering the eyes with the hand is a symbolic act of shame or embarrassment. Though symbolic, it is usually a subconscious reaction. This is significant since most people feel shame, guilt, embarrassment and/or fear when they are trying to deceive others.

When we are feeling threatened, our bodies prepare to fight or escape (the Autonomic Nervous System's fight or flight mechanism). In interview situations where deception may be an issue, the brain still subconsciously wants to respond. The response is based in a fight or flight dichotomy. When actually fleeing or fighting are not realistic options such as in interviews, we often find ourselves orienting our bodies (or its parts) toward an exit.

Alternately we may extend our legs in front of the body to serve as a barrier indicating stress - especially when we lean back to accomplish the leg extension. By leaning back, the impression is supposed convey either a carefree or an aggressive nature. Although rarely involved in deception withdrawing the main part of the body by leaning back suggests a general fear-based stress. However, if this is performed with other indicators it is reasonable to consider it support for concluding stress and fear – which can be used in the stress clustering approach in deception identification.

Keep in mind, that when something is desired, we move toward it. When we are afraid, we freeze or move away except when we are advancing toward an object of anger and in this case other bodily signals make that pretty apparent.

If those options become unrealistic and the fear continues, aggression may result, and because the bodies ANS is already activated, the shift can occur much more quickly. Imagine cornering a frightened dog, they can become aggressive in a flash.

It's important to note that juvenile and young adolescent males are an exception to some of these posturing and movement rules. During adolescence while the prefrontal cortex is restructuring, males tend to overproduce or over-react to testosterone and its by-product dihydrotestosterone (also referred to as DHT or Super Testosterone- due to its aggressive and combative response to certain behaviors – especially being disrespected in front of peers).

Testosterone and DHT may promote interpersonal and even challenging aggressiveness which is usually accompanied by their confrontational and aggressive stance and/or their use of disrespectful or challenging dialogue. As a result seeing an adolescent male extending his legs in into the space between himself and an interviewer is not uncommon.

These expressions are biological in nature and unlikely to reflect topically significant information unless they specifically occur in relation to a topic and are not the result of a perceived personally disrespectful act by the interviewer. It is also likely that this knowledge can be used in other approaches and to other ends; Such as how to reduce aggressiveness in an interaction.

# Gestures

Gestures are bodily actions and movements that communicate meaning. Some have very specific meanings, some are rather vague, and others simply describe. Many gestures are culture specific, and may be easily misinterpreted if you are unfamiliar with that culture. There are five forms of gestures: Affect Displays, Communication Supports, Manipulators, Illustrators and Emblems. Affect displays are used to indicate our emotions. Most are facial expressions, but many are found in the manner we use other parts of our bodies such as defiant hands on hips, demeaning eye rolls or shrugs of ignorance. Communication Supports are slight indications we use to determine and manipulate the flow of a conversation such as eyebrow raises as we finish a sentence indicating it is the next person's turn to speak.

## Manipulators

Manipulators are usually hand and arm activities that disperse nervous energy. They are actions used to make contact with other body parts such as in grooming actions (picking brushing, rubbing, adjusting and so on). Although these actions possess no meaning of their own, they represent discomfort when in formal situations, but they also represent considerable comfort such as when in one's own home.

When manipulators are used consistently throughout an interview, they indicate a general anxiety over the interview. When they occur in response to specific issues or questions, they serve as a possible indicator of stress in relation to that issue. In such a case, manipulating gestures regularly come in clusters and the anxiety of the specific subject can be verified by further probing on that issue, or by avoiding the issue and returning to it at a later time to see if the manipulating activities are repeated.

For example, during an interview the subject sits in a relaxed manner, moving casually on occasion. When the subject is asked about a specific topic, such as an on-the-job theft, the subject again adjusts how he sits (as he did before) but the movement occurs in conjunction with him rubbing the back of his neck, adjusting his tie, and then picking lint from his pant leg. As he begins to respond to the question, he also scratches his cheek subtly brushing the end of his nose at the same time. This suggests the subject is very nervous and even stressed about the topic.

Because manipulators use is a subconscious behavior rather than a completely unconscious (reflex-like) action, we can become aware of our use of and even exert control over them. Interview training programs often include lessons on how achieve such control and how to best present themselves when using it.

Once we are consciously aware we are using manipulators, we will usually try to extinguish them, distract from them or at least cover their presentation – especially if our need is to find relief (we all know how distracting an itch can be and how hard it is to ignore).

For example, in a stressful situation, such as an interview, when the ANS is activated, we will sense an itch coming on and when the uncontrollable urge to relieve it hits us, we disguise the act by acting out a false yawn, politely covering our mouth while incidentally rubbing the nose.

Many manipulators also make use of the face or the mouth in their actions. We see this in lip biting, cheek chewing, mouth wiping, chewing on earpieces and so on.

Even when the person is aware of this tendency, few are able to fully and convincingly control their actions. This allows us to obtain much more information about the person than they realize they are communicating. For example, they indicate discomfort as discussed, as well as shame or guilt when covering the eyes.

Manipulators are considered reliable as signs of deceit IF evaluated in as part of a cluster, tied to a particular topic and supported by other deception measures.

## Illustrators

Illustrators are actions of the arms and hands that assist the expression of a concept that is difficult to put into words -- such as defining the word zigzag, giving directions, describing an object or a landmark. Illustrators have little meaning independent of their role as a visual communications assistant.

When appropriately used illustrators can be an excellent source of additional support when coming to a conclusion of deception or honesty. Future research may reveal verification of the common assumption that they also are good honesty indicators. However, for now this is only presumed (though with many very experienced and educated advocates).

A common useful and strong indicator of deception is when the subject tries to consciously control the use of their illustrators. The resulting movements rarely match the speech, contents or intensity of the associated verbalizations.

Generally speaking, unless a deception has been well rehearsed, there will be a decrease in illustrator use when deceiving. On the other hand, illustrator use increases with increased emotional involvement, when they are truly angry, horrified, agitated, distressed, or excited. Thus if these are being shown to represent the emotional state of mind, but their presentation is improper in timing, intensity, range, location or just in violation of their baseline patterns, the illustrator likely indicates deception.

A reduction of illustrator use and extent is often associated with a lack of interest, low emotional investment, involvement, or just plain boredom. The use of illustrators also decreases when the person is thinking intently (using the internal dialogue while considering which words to use) and when such internal dialogue or concentration is unnecessary and or off the baseline (or out of character). In such situations, a conclusion of deception under construction is reasonable.

## Emblems

Emblems are gestures that have very precise meaning. As a result, they can be used effectively used without explanation.

For example, in the United States, holding one's hand above the waist with the thumb touching the forefinger in the shape of a circle and the other fingers extended and palm turned out represents the phrase "ALL OK" or "A-OK".

When an emblem is subconsciously leaked, it is often presented in partial or fragmented form (the symbol is not fully developed) and/or it isn't presented in its normal location. When "emblem leaks" occur, their inherent meaning remains the same and the meaning they communicate is very trustworthy. Because it is displayed outside the normal location or presentation area, and is only a fragment of the whole emblem, these are rarely noticed. In fact many are only identified when reviewed in a photograph or a video at some later time.

When an emblem is leaked, it can represent a deception if its meaning is contrary to what is being communicated at that time.

If other communication signals are present and they are in agreement with the emblem, the holistic message is honest. If they are not in agreement (such as one message indicating friendly while others indicate unfriendly) deception is taking place and the message communicated by the emblem is the more trustworthy.

# Vocal Indicators

Subconscious or 'paralinguistic' vocalizations provide another set of kinesic clues. Although people are very aware of the words they choose, they make many additional sounds that are not true words. These vocalizations range from unconscious reflex actions (ouch) to a conscious use of non-linguistic sounds (Hmm).

However, most indicators in this section are based on subconscious behaviors meaning we can be made aware of them and with practice, control them to a large degree. Fortunately, though most people are fully aware of them, few bother to overcome and inhibit their use.

# Speech Deviations and Errors

Analysis of vocal and speech errors is a process of determining if sounds/words used maybe valid indications of deception.

Speech and vocal errors are only significant when they deviate from the person's baseline. Presenting many speech disruptions (pauses, ums, and so on) without clear reason and when they are not a part of the baseline indicate a stalling effort to obtain additional thinking time.

Whenever an emotion is aroused, there is an impulse to make a sound. It is very difficult to keep signs of felt emotion out of the voice. For this reason, the tone, timbre and other vocal qualities rarely give false emotional messages.

Unfortunately there is insufficient research in this area to provide a complete set of descriptions as to how the voice reflects which emotion. However, one solid finding is the connection between increased pitch and deception. All other similar vocal variations are not connected (volume, speed, cracking, etc.) with deception, though they often do indicate high stress levels.

One of the most commonly accepted vocal-based indicators of deception is the presence of pauses while speaking when their baseline did not indicate that as a normal behavioral pattern for that person. This also includes the acts of stuttering, using incomplete sentences, leaving out parts of speech, difficulties in annunciation, halting speech and restarting a sentence repeatedly.

When not indicated as normal in the baseline, stuttering and annunciation difficulties indicate an effort to buy thinking time. However, it may simply indicate a question of sufficient stress or one so unexpected it mentally catches them off guard and requires additional processing (thinking) time.

As a college professor I would try to motivate my students to ask questions by reminding them of the oft used expression, "There is no such thing as a stupid question." In one such instance a student raised his hand and asked, "Dr. Camp, what is the color of the belly of an armadillo?" Given this was a sociology class, the question was so far outside my expectations I had to take a moment to process the paradigm shift before trying to answer in some manner that would eliminate me retracting my claim about stupid questions. Note: I failed and announced, "Maybe there are some questions that would be stupid in a given situation."

These same stalling issues apply to halting speech (stopping and starting as they construct portions of a sentence) as well as a subject repeatedly starting the same sentence.

Many people, especially Americans, are uncomfortable with silence. When we are constructing a response that requires 'dead time' we tend to fill those gaps with some kind of sound. The result is that when we are thinking of a response, inserting a speech error (even subconsciously) or a paralinguistic sound allows us to avoid the silent moment while avoiding the necessity of giving away the need to contrive or edit an answer.

In this light we must be aware of the questions we ask (see interviewing). Some questions simply require more thought. For example, asking, "did you work the last shift at the store last night" should require virtually no time in responding. On the other hand, "what did you do after cashing out before locking up?" requires the person to take the time to re-live the situation (especially if there were multiple actions taken).

Similarly, if a question is confusing in how it is asked, it may take time to identify the point of the question before an answer can be provided. For example asking, "Why do you feel medical use of marijuana is not an issue of legality but an issue of the people who are not in need of medical marijuana when there are other available drugs they can already get if they see the right doctor?" This could simply be asked as, "What are your views on medical marijuana?"

Other speech errors include incomplete sentences, sentences that are missing parts of speech, change in vocal pitch (deceptive comments often come with a higher than baseline vocal pitch.

When a person does not complete his or her sentences and that behavior is not seen in the baseline setting, it can indicate a stress based issue. When people are faced with a challenging question that requires extra thought and they do not stall for time, they will often speak as they think. When doing so, if the topic is concerning to them (stressor), they may place greater emphasis on thinking over responding. The result is often that expected parts of the sentence are left out.

Another perspective is that if a sentence is incomplete, the subject is subconsciously indicating less faith in what they are saying. This is particularly true when leaving out important items such as pronouns, especially "I". Missing parts of speech are covered in depth under Discourse or Content Analysis.

As previously suggested, an increased vocal pitch indicates strong emotion, stress and is significantly correlated with deception. When we feel stress, our vocal chords tighten causing our pitch to increase. Determining if indicators of other emotions are present should be made (such as fear, surprise or anger) as they may suggest alternative reasons for the vocal variation.

While Expression Analysis determines which emotion is presently felt, we can make some assumptions: If the source emotion is anger, efforts to de-escalate the emotion are in order and other signs of ANS activation should be evident. If the anger is falsely being presented, the person is being deceptive. If the emotion is surprise, the reaction should be clear based on expression analysis criteria such as the fact that expressions of true surprise are very short lived – a mere few seconds AT MOST.

If the emotion is fear, remember that fear is the basis for deception and a change in pitch is very likely related to deceit. Using multiple indicators as in this situation will greatly help determine the nature of the interaction. If there is no reason for deception then determining the source of the fear should become the focus.

Although it is claimed subconscious behaviors are more reliable behavioral indicators than our other available forms of interpersonal communication, the behaviors of the subconscious can be largely controlled. While most people are not able to accomplish this realistically, it is possible to a large degree once we are aware of them. Ultimately, the degree of agreement between these behaviors and the other modes of communication is the best measure of deception and honesty.

# Internal Dialogue

The **Internal Dialogue** is the process of turning our mental focus inward. When we do this, we become less aware of the surroundings and often stare off into the distance which provides a listless or spaced-out appearance.

Humans are quite poor at true mental multitasking. What we are good at (at least some of us) is very rapidly switching between one task and another. To illustrate this inability try this: add three simple numbers together (5, 17, and 6) and subtract three different numbers from one another (28-3-13) AT THE SAME TIME. Not only can you not do this, you cannot do either task all at once. You would add 5 to 17 and then add the additional 6 to that sum. Similarly you would do the subtraction one number at a time.

While most of us can walk and think at the same time, common behaviors such as driving show that when the subconscious behavior requires conscious attention (such as a car unexpectedly stopping in front of us) our actions must require our full attention. A multitude of studies on drivers using their cell phones (even hands free) reveal this as fact. However, that being the case, it is still possible that people can carry out physical actions as though they are reflexive if they have performed them so much the action seems to require no mental effort.

Recognizing the signs of a person turning to their internal dialogue is very important. When we recall an actual memory, that act rarely demands much in the way of mental processing. If the request is a rather simply request, recall is usually immediate and often comes to mind with numerous minute and specific details. For example, recall what you had for breakfast this morning or recall the last time you went shopping. How long did it take and how many details (especially emotions, sensations, and feelings in general) came to mind almost immediately?

When a person recalling what should be a simple memory but they take an unusually long in recalling that memory, he or she is editing their answer before stating it. Because "Everything we do we do for a reason", we must ask, "Why did the subject need to edit THAT specific response?" If there is no clear and rational reason for such an extra mental step (it was years ago, or I was drunk), this is a sign they are very likely preparing a deceptive response by editing out specific information. Information they would prefer not to share.

This can be further determined by the quality and depth of their response, use of other detection modes, and a determination of how they normally access their internal dialogue (as determined from a baseline setting). Unless they are doing this as a determined normal behavior, they are most likely in the process of creating a deception.

Being able to spot the beginning of this type of 'thinking effort' when atypical for that person can allow us to predict and inhibit the formation of a deception before they could complete the process.

To inhibit the deception, interrupt their thinking process with a question to clarify some point previously discussed or ask an unexpected relevant question. This forces a refocus of their attention. One psychologist friend uses his body movement to refocus someone's attention once he sees they have mentally turned inward will determine where they are pointing their eyes and move into their direct line of sight reclaiming their attention and interfering with their internalized dialogue. This action immediately commands their attention and its effect is very important because once a person deceives, they are much more unlikely to admit their deception.

# Graphology (Handwriting) Analysis

**Graphology** (the study of handwriting characteristics) has been long viewed as a possible approach for deception detection. While many people believe that one's personality can be intimately dissected from an analysis of their handwriting characteristics, there is little if any objective research support for this belief. However, there are three uses involving handwriting in deception identification that have significant research support and valid theoretical foundations: Signature Forgery, Stress Analysis, and Mental Processing.

Expert forgery analysts tell us that people can change the superficial aspects of their writing, but few are able to alter the more subtle characteristics. Those trained in signature analysis are primarily involved in signature comparisons with the goal of identifying forged signatures. Identification of a forged signature is vitally important in issues such as contesting wills. These expert graphologists look at writing elements such as slant (slope), size, thickness, pressure, organization, spacing, letter formation, connections, final and initial strokes, and consistency of style from start to finish. When significant variations from a verified signature exist, the authenticity of that signature is in question.

The second application of handwriting analysis is that of stress identification. When experiencing stress, the body undergoes a marked increase in adrenaline. When something written has indications of increased pressure, it is thought that the increased pressure is the result of increased stress, possibly caused by deception.

Some evaluators would determine the stress by having the written statement (or job application) conducted on a pad of paper with a hard point pen. The reviewer could examine the back side of the paper for indications of excessive pressure; specifically, the greater the stress at a given point in the statement (as in responding to a sensitive question), the greater the indentation into the paper and the larger the resulting 'hump' on the reverse side. While this is definitely indication of greater pressure, it is only suggestive of increased stress.

As with all stress indicators, the presence of stress does not equal deception, but since it is an indicator, the content of what is written at those sites (increased pressure indicators) can provide a narrowing of specific points to focus on during follow-up interviews or investigations.

Another use of handwriting analysis is to indicate mental involvement. When we are honest, we rarely require significant mental effort when writing a simple recollection. However, when we deceive, we normally pause to mentally produce our fabrication (whether the deception is careful editing or total fabrication).

When the flow of the statement is consistent, the style is uninterrupted and also is consistent. However, when pausing to reflect on what to write, the flow is interrupted giving clues as to what content items need closer consideration. After the subject determines what to include or how to phrase what they wish to include, they will resume the writing. This pause causes a slight change in writing characteristics. Combining the pressure indicators and style changes can indicate where concerning information is located within the written statement give focus for interview questions or for a follow-up investigation.

Another indicator some use is the blob mark of where a person has been resting the point of an ink pen while thinking. When the tip of the pen rests on the paper, which is usually where the person paused to think, the ink wicks out onto the paper at that spot creating a small ink spot.

For example, when a subject is writing about the morning bathroom rituals (shower, shave, etc.) then has an ink blob just before dressing, it may suggest that the blob was where the pen was being rested while the subject thought over the events that occurred at that point in the morning ritual. The investigator would have to consider 'What events in that setting require mental filtering?' Most people would just say something like, "and then got dressed . . .' rather than taking a pause to decide what to say at that point. In many instances this is completely meaningless, but at other times, this will direct the focus of concern for gaining more information.

Another indicator to watch for is how the writing space is used. When a subject uses larger than typical spacing, letters, punctuation, marked out words, and filler, they give the appearance of being fully cooperative (they filled out the entire space allowed) while being able to avoid sensitive or stressful information simply because they 'ran out of room'.

Graphology is most useful as an indicator of stress or pointing out a change in thinking patterns (which may or may not indicate deception). By using those indicators, the interviewer is able to identify specific directions of inquiry that may be otherwise overlooked or hidden in an effort to cover ever avenue of investigation due to a lack of evidence based focus.

# 6 CONSCIOUS BEHAVIORS

While kinesics can identify stress from deception, there are other stress based behaviors that are consciously produced. These purposeful behavioral changes supplement deception by avoiding specific topics, using carefully worded responses, redirecting subject matter and even intimidation.

Several training programs suggest that specific conscious actions are direct evidence of deception. However, unless supported with other indicators, there is a significant chance that conclusion is wrong. Again, the best way to determine deception is through multiple indicators and multiple methods of analysis.

For example, one such behavior is asking a "What If" question. In a situation where a crime suspect asks, "What if I am found guilty? What will happen then?" The "What if" question gives the impression the subject is not claiming responsibility, but simply wants to know what they may be facing, 'just in case'. Many programs teach that only the guilty would ask this question, and since the innocent believe they will be vindicated by the truth, they would never consider the issue. This is false. In fact there are many reasons the innocent may ask this question:

1. They have a low self-esteem.
2. They have little faith in the criminal justice system.
3. They believe prejudice or some other similar issue might result in being railroaded in court and found guilty.

However, in a situation where a baseline can be established, these alternative possibilities can be identified during the baseline setting process.

As indicated above, some verbal indicators are purposefully used to gain thinking time for deception creation. For example, the normally subconscious "uhs," "umms," and surprise vocalizations can be used consciously to this end.

When a subject seems stuck for words, he or she is trying to think of the precise words to properly reflect their intended meaning. The manner a person speaks (including careful word selection) should be identified during baseline setting. If this behavior is not identified as normal action for this person, it is probably meaningful. If it occurs with specific subjects, it indicates a serious concern about those subjects. When encountered, carefully scrutinize all their behaviors for additional indicators of deception and any hidden meanings before jumping to any conclusions.

## Controlling Behaviors

Intentionally conceived, consciously controlled behaviors are efforts to deceive or are efforts to otherwise manipulate control away from the interviewer. Generally, controlling behaviors can be divided into sections according to intent: Intimidation Tactics, Kinesic Control Efforts, Interview Hijacking, Excessive Attentiveness, and Response Manipulation.

All identified control approaches should immediately elicit the question, "given the circumstances, why does the subject feel the need to manipulate the situation at this point?" Until the reason is clearly identified such control efforts must be considered and as an indicator of deception. If a cluster of indicators is revealed, then the conclusion of deception has supportable merit and further investigation on those topics should follow.

### Intimidation

#### Name Dropping

A very common control tactic is trying to intimidate the interviewer. The goal is to get the interviewer sidetracked by suggesting the subject wields power and influence.

For example, claiming, "I'm the mayor's brother" or "I'm a personal friend of the governor" are efforts to refocus the interview by name dropping. If faced with a name dropper, ask yourself, "Why do they feel the need to be dropping names?" The most likely answer is 'they are fearful that if the interviewer maintains control over the interactional process something they don't want revealed may come to light'.

**Faked Anger**

Another approach is the use of fake anger. Because most people are intimidated when confronted with anger, this approach is often used, especially since it has a history and logic of being a successful way to manipulate behavior (think bully).

Successful management of this tactic involves identifying whether the anger is a felt (real) emotion or if it is fabricated for the purpose of redirecting the interview. Once you determine the validity of the anger, deal with it accordingly.

When a person is truly angry he or she will exhibit the signs discussed in Expression Analysis. If they do, they will normally respond to appropriate anger de-escalation techniques. Those with true 'felt' anger will often de-escalate their indicators of anger if a sincere apology is made. For example by stating, "Everyone being interviewed is being asked these same questions" or "I'm sorry this is upsetting, but it is my job" or "this must be done because other people's safety is at risk".

Alternately, faked anger is produced as a means to serve a purpose – specifically to obtain control, intimidate, and/or cause a change of topic. If fake anger is used, the subject will remain angry despite de-escalation. They may even escalate the intensity of the apparent anger until they get their desired result.

# Kinesic Control

Another technique to gain control in the interview process is more passive. Many people are aware that body language can reveal information that the interviewee is afraid of revealing. Body language has become such a common and well-known subject that many people go to great lengths to present a false impression.

These deceptive efforts are easily defeated because of the great number of ways our body communicates. This is easily identified since the subject appears abnormally stiff. While they may not give body language signals in the normal manner, the 'freezing of the body' suggests fear of being read or letting something slip. Any effort to freeze bodily action is an indicator this person is fearful of being read.

Regardless, even when the person is 'frozen', indicators and signs are still available. For instance, what was the position they choose to freeze in – defensive, relaxed, turned away, etc.

Other efforts to control the various signals of body language produce a basic problem for the subject and an opportunity for the interviewer. When trying to control the multitude of signals needed to provide a believable bodily language presentation, the task is similar to trying to catch and contain several frogs in a small bucket. Each time you raise the lid to add another captured frog, some of those inside try to escape while the lid is up. These escaping frogs are analogous to kinesic leaks – body language signals that do not fit the desired presentation goal. Regardless of our efforts, this is a massive multitasking effort and as such virtually no one can consciously control all of them at once. Doing so results in one or more kinesic leaks that are identifiable to the observant.

## Interview Hijacking

Interview hijacking is action of a subject trying to take control of the interview itself. The goal of this control tactic is to become the interviewer so they can direct the interaction that takes place. This allows the subject to avoid lying and possibly escape deception altogether by circumventing concerning topics.

## Excessive Attentiveness

The last of the commonly used control techniques is 'excessive attentiveness'. This refers to those who show an abnormal interest, curiousness, or 'helpfulness' concerning the interview or investigation.

When a subject repeatedly seeks information beyond their needs, they may be trying to gauge how much and what information has been gained to determine their level of risk.

Although some are merely interested; others have a seriously vested interest because they are involved. Getting that 'extra' information, allows them the ability to consider future events and prepare potential responses.

As we will see in the interviewing section, an interview begins when the interviewee becomes aware of whom and what they need to be paying attention to in order to have the advantage.

To discern between the abnormally curious but honest person and the deceptive person, request their help. While both will willingly cooperate, the honest person will typically offer help that is designed to narrow the investigation (even if they are way off target, the purpose is to determine their goal, not use their information). On the other hand, the person with an ulterior motive (such as deceit) will offer assistance, but in doing so he or she may broaden the scope of the investigation, provide rationale that would lead away from them, or provide other clues to suggest they may be a person of interest. They may also slip up and provide information they do not intend. As always, support any conclusions with a cluster of additional indicators and approaches.

## Response Manipulation

Another deception ploy lies in the manipulation of how a question is answered. The subject can stall for thinking time, qualify his or her answer with an escape clause, or provide an answer that only seems to answer the questions, but does not actually do so. These techniques avoid total honesty as well as stall for more thinking time.

### Stalling

**Stalling** is an act or behavior whose goal is to covertly gain additional thinking time. Baseline setting will identify whether their actions are stalling style tactics or normal behaviors for them.

Although the tactics than can be used here are almost infinite, those most often used include: false reflection, presenting the appearance of careful consideration, slowing the pace of their speech, and speech errors along with the various areas explored in the following sections.

Appearing to sincerely contemplate the question at hand allows the subject thinking time while they give the subject matter serious thought.

By using body gestures such as manipulations of the face, head and/or neck (rubbing, scratching, picking, scratching their head, rubbing their mouth, stroking their chin, etc.) they provide a facade of making a real effort to provide a well thought out answer. This is, in fact, what they are doing except their answer will be an effort to mislead.

Although a sincere person may also give this appearance, their goal is to be of real help if they can. The use of expression and gesture analysis will help determine the validity of their effort.

Another common tactic to gain thinking time is to slow down the rate of speech, slowing how fast they speak. This is easy to identify as the baseline and all interactions up to this point should demonstrate their normal pace of speaking.

Speech errors were previously discussed since they seem to lie somewhere between conscious and subconscious responses. If they are conscious, their primary goal is gain thinking time by delaying responses. Since uncharacteristic stalling normally indicates a fear of answering honestly, interrupting with truth elicitation techniques may be effective in obtaining honest responses. When delays are not conscious actions, they should be considered as a subconscious action and analyzed accordingly (see subconscious analysis).

## Qualified Response

A **qualified response** (also known as a safe out or a verbal escape clause) is a response containing one or more added phrases that give the subject the opportunity to deny responsibility for information they provided.

The following are examples of qualifier phrases: "to the best of my knowledge", "as far as I can remember", "I am almost sure that...", "I'm not sure, but...", "I think", "As far as I could tell"; "I could be wrong, but..."; "As far as I know", etc... Each one allows the subject to later escape responsibility for their statements by claiming, "I told you I wasn't sure".

When a qualifier is included, the integrity of the response is weakened. For example, in the comment, "There is no real threat" the message perceived is seen as more reliable than, "As far as I know, there is no real threat."

When a qualifier is encountered, you should ask yourself, "Why is that safety phrase needed?" and "What made them feel the need to be cautious in this particular comment?"

If the person's baseline did not involve qualifier-type thinking, using a qualifier may indicate deception. **Qualifier-type thinking** refers to the thinking process of a person who habitually qualifies what they say in an effort to be precise or in those with a low self-esteem, as a safety against the possibility of being wrong.

## Response Avoidance

Potentially the most common manipulation technique used to deceive is to avoid answering the question 'exactly as it was asked'. By carefully selecting the wording of their response, the deceptive respondent can provide what superficially appears to be a relevant and appropriate answer to the question asked. However, the response actually answers a slightly different question than what was asked.

Example: Investigating a violent crime against a woman, her ex-husband, the suspect, is asked "Who did you see last night?" He answers, "I didn't see nobody yesterday!" This answer may mean he defined her as nobody, he may be relying on the double negative to disguise that he did see someone but did not answer the question, or he may have seen her last night, but not during the day.

Another tactic used to avoid answering the question is to begin an answer then redirect its focus by rambling into unrelated areas.

# Rambling

**Rambling** is the practice of stalling by talking extensively and continuously, but effectively offering nothing useful and not answering the question. When a rambler is performing their extensive and wide ranging response dialogue, they will also be mentally searching for a good way to further respond, alter the topic or manage some other type of misdirection.

Meanwhile they might also be hoping the lengthy and pointless response will satisfy the needs of the interviewer as if they in fact gave the needed response.

Alternately they may hope the interviewer will tire and move on. They may also conclude from the mass of information that this subject is offering lots of information out of a sincere desire to cooperate but decide they are not of any further interest with respect to the investigation.

The following is an example of how this might be carried out:

> What was I doing last night? Well that's a question. I was doing a lot of things. How detailed do you want? Do you want to know about while washing clothes the lint trap almost catching fire? It's a good thing I keep a fire extinguisher in the laundry room. Or, do you want to know who came to visit? I have lots of friends that often drop by without phoning ahead...

Other than using a baseline comparison and indicator clustering, it is possible to distinguish between the deceptive and the honest rambler by seeking to refocus their attention. Politely announcing the need for effective use of time followed by a restating of the question should get a straightforward response free of deception indicators, a deceptive response or another diversion.

Another common method is to change the topic. When asked, 'Where were you last night?' a subject responds with:

"Where was I last night?, well usually on Monday, I go shopping, you know the store always has soda on sale if you get there right after the manager leaves, and since I drink a lot of soda that's important to me. Speaking of that, would you care for a drink? You know, people are not as appropriate to guests as they once were. Do you find that people are rude to you a lot?"

The Deception Management solution is to pay close attention to the response and if it is a 'question avoidance' effort, either note it for later consideration or confront them and seek a more honest response.

Be aware that if you confront them, you will weaken rapport since they will recognize that you did not accept their deception tactic. To minimize the rapport loss when confronting them, simply and politely thank them for their answer and then indicate how their response did not answer the question and restate the question.

When someone does not answer a question as it was asked, either they did not understand the question or they are trying to avoid answering it. Make sure your questions are properly asked before assuming the other person is trying to be deceptive.

# Excuses

**Excuses** are behaviors designed to produce a conclusion that this person has no involvement or no accountability if they were involved: in other words, 'this is not a person of interest concerning the topic at hand'. When a person has a fear of being held accountable for something, they will often seek avenues of escape. In this section, the escape effort is to avoid being identified as a person of interest. Escape efforts include: Denials, Objections, and Appeals to Higher Authorities or to strong moral convictions.

# Denials

In general, **denials** are statements intended to claim, "I didn't do it". Denials are normal and expected reactions to accusations. Rejecting an accusation is almost a survival trait that we should expect.

## Types of Denials

Denials come in a variety of styles. Among the myriad forms are the straight forward denials, specific denials, non-verbal denials, and denials demonstrated by inappropriate affect and action.

The **straight forward denial** is the one and only denial generally considered as honest. The straight forward denial is often a literal, "I didn't do it!"

Other denials are manipulative efforts that seem to claim innocence but are actually efforts to deceptively mislead. Because people prefer not to lie (in the absence of special considerations) the guilty will often use these alternatives.

**Specific (limited) denials** make use of interviewer error and/or semantic manipulation (using very specific definitions) based on minor factual errors concerning the topic in question. For example, a subject was arrested for selling 31 and 2/3 ounces of marijuana (1.9 pounds). When the interviewer asked the suspect about selling of the 2 pounds (32 ounces) of marijuana, he was able to truthfully, adamantly and with conviction deny that he did not possess, own or sell 2 pounds of marijuana.

Another similar denial is to mentally (but non-verbally) add to their response a thought or comment that makes the response true. For instance, when selling the 1.9 pounds of marijuana, he denied the accusation in a manner that indicated honesty. He said, "I did not sell anything." However, mentally he added, "I traded it for money, I'm no salesman".

Because these denials are not actual lies, stress indicators are frequently less obvious or absent, making stress based analysis potentially less effective. In the subject's mind they are being fully truthful. Another tactic used with specific denials is the use of errors – errors in time, place date, and circumstances. Watch for efforts to include specific details in denial statements.

Another type of denial uses expressions of oath, honesty, religiosity, position and integrity to insinuate their denial is valid. These include expressions such as: Honestly, Frankly, "I am being as honest as I can", 'I am serious as a heart attack' 'I swear to God' and so on. However, these must be considered in light of their overall demeanor and psychological makeup.

For example, a person that is easily intimidated, has a low self-esteem, or has high respect for authority and does not feel comfortable correcting authority figures may feel the need to add these forms of support to emphasize how strongly they are denying the accusation. In these cases the denial may in fact be quite accurate.

## Taking Advantage of Denials

If you know facts related to the interview, and also know the subject is unaware of them, you can use them by asking about them in a way that suggests you do not have that answer. Their answer will either coincide with your hidden, known facts or they will not, indicating deception. Once they are caught in the deception (about these incidental facts) the subject will have less faith in their ability to deceive the interrogator.

Another similar tactic is the use of false facts. If a subject claims to have gone to Harvard business school, and you have a gut feeling that they are lying, ask them a question such as, "I see you graduated in 1994, the year Dr. Harold won the Ulrich Peace prize. Were you one of the students that got to go to his social event and meet Bill Gates?"

Since there was no such situation, a real graduate would most likely state something to clear that up. Those that did not attend Harvard, would not know how to respond and would likely make up an answer that would be obvious.

# Objections

Whereas a denial is a statement of: "I didn't do it." An **objection** serves to provide a seemingly rational explanation as to "why they could not have been the person that did it."

They are trying to offer why something cannot be true. Objections are statements of, "I couldn't have done it. Here is why!" As a rule objections usually follow a denial as a means to strengthen the validity of the denial.

There are two main categories of objections: circumstance based (the facts don't fit) and personal traits based (I'm not the kind of person that could do it). Personal trait objections may consist of either emotional objections (I'm afraid of guns) or moral (I am a God fearing person who would never do such a thing) or both.

Examples – An Honest Objection: "I did not take the money and I could not have because I was in class and I can prove it because the teacher took attendance."

A 'Likely Deception': "I have never used a drug like meth, besides I have a heart condition, if I did something like that, I would be risking my life".

Some training programs suggest that an objection itself is reason to consider a person as potentially deceptive. However, this approach ignores the intimidation factor of being asked and the potential of low self-esteem. When people feel that those asking questions deserve greater respect (or they fear them because of their status) they are likely to try to re-enforce their comments to assure the response is taken seriously. The Deception Management approach to defeat this is:

1. Establish the self-esteem issue during the baseline setting. Their demeanor should present this clearly.
2. Rely on clusters from other approaches. Deceptive objections are usually highlighted with clusters of additional deception indicators.
3. Verify the information. When objections are based on objective circumstances –witnesses or other verifiable evidence - the objection can be useful in identifying previously overlooked facts or considerations.

**Note**: When an objection fails, the subject is likely to respond with either anger or defeat.

Consider the objection in the following real life example from the case files of the famous Elias Parker. Parker was a famed and exceptional investigator of Burlington County New Jersey, was known worldwide as the Sherlock Holmes of America.

In the famous "Ellis Parker and the Pickled Corpse Case", Parker felt the objection of a suspect seemed problematic, although it was verifiable. The suspected man could not have been at the murder scene at the estimated time of death. Adjusting his considerations on the concept that there must be another variable, Ellis rechecked the facts and discovered that the body had been found soaked in water under an oak tree.

Through a process of deduction and research, he found that oak tainted waters at the death scene had 'pickled' the body and the initial estimated time of death was incorrect. With the new information, a new time of death was determined and the 'objecting' suspect no longer had an alibi. When confronted, he confessed.

## Conclusions and Summary

In general, when a person is aware (conscious) of their actions and are trying to derail an avenue of investigation, they are being deceptive. However, even when someone is consciously deceiving, that act alone cannot directly inform people as to what the honest truth of the situation is. You must utilize all the methods of investigation to arrive at the most reliable and valid determination of deception and its specific cause.

# 7 EXPRESSION ANALYSIS

Emotions are mental states. They are a combination of our perceptions and our reflections on our perceptions. Emotions are expressed throughout a person's body, but especially so with facial muscles.

Expression Analysis is based on the presence of seven basic and universally recognized emotions and their accompanying expressions. Based on the vast research findings of Dr. Paul Ekman (one of the 100 most eminent psychologists of the twentieth century), his colleagues and students these findings have incredible amounts of verified support. One conclusion resulting from these studies is that Expression Analysis is presently the most effective single mode approach for detecting deception.

Among his many research findings were the identification of 'naturals' – about 3 in a 1000 people who are naturally gifted at correctly evaluating deception. When these 'naturals' (AKA wizards) were asked how they go about reaching their conclusions, in summary they said they recognize base their conclusions on recognizing when a person's various forms of interpersonal communications are mismatched or out of sync.' Expressions are the most common basis for their comparisons.

## Using Expressions in Analysis

Two ways expressions can be used for deception analysis:
1. Identification of Repressed and False Expressions
2. Multi-Modal/Multi- Channel Comparisons

# Identification of Deceptive Expressions

## Repressed Expressions

A repressed or **squelched expression** is a true expression that when consciously recognized, is interrupted and diminished, removed or replaced. The very act of trying to conceal an expression is deception with respect to their actual feelings.

## Micro Expressions

A **micro-expression** is a fully expressed emotion that lasts often much less than ½ second before being repressed. Micro-expressions are very reliable as a measure of a true, felt emotion. When micro expressions indicate one emotion, but other signals disagree, the micro-expression is the more reliable and valid signal. In such a case, when signals disagree, deception is usually taking place.

When we first experience an emotion, that information is handled by our amygdala which relays a command to the facial muscles to express the emotion accordingly. At the same time, the amygdala also sends that information to the thinking and rational prefrontal cortex. These signals arrive at their destination (face versus pre-frontal cortex) at different speeds with the face being the first to get and respond to the emotion resulting in the associated expression. This produces an expression that is displayed for about ¼ second before we are rationally aware of the emotion and can afford some control over it. This means that expressions reflect actual emotion felt for about ¼ second before we become aware of it and can gain control over the expression. Once we have control we can choose to manipulate the expression if desired. The most common manipulation is to replace the emotionally based expression with one that is consciously fabricated.

Although there is only a brief fraction of a second before the real emotion can be masked, in that brief moment, the true felt emotion can be identified by learning to recognize the expressions that go with those universal emotions. With a little training and practice, it is possible to identify what a person is actually feeling, regardless of their desire to mask their feelings.

# Subtle Expressions

Subtle Expression Analysis is similar to micro-expression analysis with a few important differences. A subtle expression lasts longer than a micro-expression but is presented in reduced fashion. Dr. David Matsumoto defines subtle expressions as "expressions that occur when a person is just starting to feel an emotion, or when their emotional response to a situation, another person or the environment around them is of low intensity." However, Dr. Paul Ekman has a slightly different view. He suggests that a diminished (subtle expression) may be low intensity, remnants of a strong expression or an expression that is not truly felt. They are often fragments of a full expression (involving just a part of the face) or they are significantly reduced in intensity. This often occurs when a subject becomes aware of their presence and consciously tries to 'squelch the expression.

Although it is not verified, it is possible that these are not independent views but are both correct. The micro expression is less common and more difficult to identify because of its rapid removal from the face. Subtle expressions may be less accurate because of the low level intensity or the invalidity due to being suppressed, but the longer lasting effect, and the inability of many people to completely wipe an expression from the face makes this more likely to be usable across a greater spectrum of situations.

Normally such efforts cannot erase all of the felt expression leaving remnants of the true felt emotion. While identification is more difficult due to reduced intensity and fragmentation, the presentation lasts longer than micro- expressions.

Deception may be indicated in two ways. When the subtle expression remains at a reduced intensity, but the existence of strong emotion is otherwise indicated or when an expression is replaced with a false expression to consciously conceal the true felt emotion.

# Asymmetrical Expressions

An **asymmetrical expression** is an expression that is presented more strongly on one side of the face than the other. Like masked expressions, asymmetrical expressions are usually false.

Most people are able to identify expression asymmetry far better than chance making asymmetry a strong and valid indicator of a deceptive expression.

The two exceptions to this are the contempt expression which is solely expressed on one side of the face and the "I don't have a clue" expression which is similar to the contempt, but is an asymmetrical expression that is very similar in appearance to contempt, but is combined with a shoulder shrug and usually extended arms with upturned palms (see contempt).

## Expression Masking (False Expressions)

When choosing to mask (hide) a felt expression, the most common expression used is the false smile. Others used include expressions of anger or more rarely, a neutral expression (the true poker face).

Usually when masking an expression, individuals also try to control every other aspect of their appearance causing a frozen unnatural appearance and awkward appearing or jerky movements.

A false smile, being the most common cover or mask can be identified by a failure to lower the eyebrow near the inner part of the eyelid (caused by an unconscious and uncontrollable tightening of that part of the upper eyelid). This false smile is especially recognizable when it is presented in an inappropriate situation and when the offset time is abnormal. If an expression is of long duration (five or more seconds) it is likely to be a false or mock expression or an emblem conveying a very specific and clear message.

Also, while regaining control over expressions can occur in a fraction of a second, regaining full vocal control of associated vocal characteristics, such as the increased vocal pitch of fear takes as much as 5 full seconds.

To use either approach you must learn to accurately identify what the expressions represent AND you must become proficient in reading and interpreting demeanor, body language and verbal communications.

# Multimodal Comparisons

When deception indicators are identified by any one technique, the best results possible are 70% or less (usually less).

However, when a person uses multiple techniques in analyzing indicators and then compares them to one another (the multi-modal approach) research has produced success rates of over 90%.

Unfortunately, most training in any one of the techniques requires extensive knowledge to achieve those 'best' results. The Multimodal training in Deception Management has been able to reduce the amount of information necessary to learn each of the various techniques.

Although reducing the amount of training in a technique does not achieve the very top success level for that technique, research has shown the minute details of each technique are not necessary for them to be effective. This allows the trainee to gain the most important aspects of each method in a short amount of time by cutting the 'fat' that is only useful in highly specialized situations.

Since the goal of multimodal training is to find the most effective aspects of each and merge them, the trainee can master the basics of several approaches thereby achieving high success rates without the enormous amounts of time and effort normally involved with in-depth learning of a single technique.

# Emotions and Their Expressions

Recognizing 'felt' emotions requires close visual observation of facial expressions. To identify felt emotions we must learn to distinguish one emotion from another by its associated expression. There are two ways to accomplish this: identification in a fraction of a second (see micro-expressions) or by identification based on expressions that are significantly reduced in intensity (see subtle expressions).

While most people have been taught the differences between various expressions through the socialization process and practice, becoming proficient at using these approaches requires learning to consistently and correctly identify the emotion causing the expression. This is accomplished through learning minute facial muscle actions and movements. While being a true expert requires extensive knowledge, following a very few basic rules allows virtually anyone can become fairly proficient.

To achieve this ability we need to learn the more common and useful expressions, what muscle actions indicate them, variations of expression and the basics in using Expression Analysis.

There are seven general categories of emotion, each one representing a large number of potential variations. Learning to identify the facial expressions of these seven categories will provide the basis for recognizing virtually all human emotions. The seven basic emotions are: Fear, Anger, Contempt, Disgust, Surprise, Sadness and Happiness.

Each of the following sections will provide information for recognizing and understanding each category of emotions.

## Fear

Although anger is considered a more powerful and dangerous emotion, fear is the most dominating of emotions. Fear drives behavior more than any other emotion. Fear is also the cause for most deception. In determining if a person is being deceptive, the majority of experts in the area of lie detecting seek indicators of fear (stress indicators) to identify likely deception. Unfortunately, these approaches seek stress to indicate fear. Because fear is only one source of stress, using stress as the primary indicator is why lie detectors, such as the polygraph, tend to be limited in their ability to detect deception. This is why they are not allowed in most courts.

Although fear and the associated stress provide many biological and behavioral indicators, the facial expression of fear is distinctive. As a result the best approach to identify fear is to identify the facial expression that represents fear and fear alone.

The signs or indicators of the fear expression include raised eyebrows that are pulled together combined with raised upper eyelids, tensed lower eyelids and lips that are stretched horizontally and backward toward the ears. As with all indicators, never presume fear equals deception. While it very well might, there are many people experiencing fear that are not deceptive at that moment. Making a conclusion of deception is best if based on additional verification through clusters of repeated and multiple indicators.

## Anger

Anger is an emotional response that often occurs when there is interference with what people are doing. Anger is considered the most dangerous emotion, not because of the negative aspects it possesses, but because observing anger invokes the brain of the observer to also feel anger which results in the potential of anger escalation.

The best approach in interacting with an angry person is to acknowledge and if possible, defuse the cause of the anger rather than confront or argue.

Signs of anger include glaring eyes (raised upper eyelids and tightened lower eyelids) with the lowered, drawn together, eyebrows and tightened, pressed lips causing the red margins of the lips to appear thinner. The pressing or narrowing of the lips is one of the most reliable signs of felt anger. However, if the facial signs (eyebrows and pressed lips) occur without glaring eyes, this is an expression of intense mental focus or concentration.

Real anger increases blood flow to the upper body, arms and hands. Commonly the jaw is thrust forward and behaviorally there is an impulse to move toward the target of anger using a confrontational style of body language.

## Contempt

Contempt indicates a lack of respect and is often combined with a feeling of intense dislike and even anger. Contempt expresses power, status and a feeling of superiority (associated with disapproval toward others) and conveys beliefs such as, "I have one over on you" or "I am better than you" or "I do not agree or approve of, or with, you".

The expression of contempt is identified by lifting and tightening the lips on one side of the mouth. It is the only expression that is always and only unilateral (shown only on one side of the face). Behaviorally there is an impulse to look down on the object of contempt. Contempt shown within a relationship often represents a troubled relationship.

However, contempt can be confused with a partial smile (but lacks the rest of the facial indicators of happiness) or a sign of uncertainty (if combined with shrug gesture and raised eyebrows).

The main difference between contempt and felt smile is the tightened lip corner present in contempt, but absent in the felt smile and a partial smile will still exhibit some muscle tension bilaterally (across both sides of the face with one side being dominant).

It is also important to note that contempt generally reflects a negative emotion. As a result, while contempt may be felt and expressed alone, it is frequently accompanied by either anger or disgust.

## Surprise

Surprise is the briefest emotion and occurs when a person is 'very' suddenly exposed to something unexpected.

The main recognizing features are the jaw dropping down causing the mouth to open, forming an "O" shape, while the eyes widen and the eyebrows rise without being pulled together. If the signs last longer than the briefest of times (i.e. prolonged "O" shape) the expression is a deception

This is a valuable emotion to recognize and watch for when presenting information for the first time (prices, judgments, bids, news, etc.) since its characteristics allow an evaluation as to whether the information is truly surprising and new.

## Disgust

Disgust is the emotion felt when a person encounters or considers something offending repulsive and thought of as distasteful, repugnant, and nauseating and so on. It is generally considered that the most potent and common triggers of disgust bodily materials we expel such as feces, vomit, urine, mucus and infectious materials and blood.

There are two facial expressions that indicate disgust: nose wrinkling and raising the upper lip. Either one indicates disgust, but they often occur together. When intense disgust is felt, the person often lowers the eyebrows as we wrinkle the nose. This can be mistaken for anger except that the brows and the upper eye lids do not rise. Sometimes disgust may be unilateral signaling a combination with contempt.

## Sadness

Sadness is one of the longer lasting emotions and is the result of feeling hopelessness, resignation or loss. Because sadness is a passive emotion, it is less likely to convert to anger or another more action based emotion.

The most reliable sign of sadness is the raised inner corners of the eyebrows that cause the eyebrows to appear as if they are drawn on an angle (lower on the outside and upward near the inner corners). This often produces a vertical wrinkle between brows. A downward stare or gazing is also typical. The lip corners are pulled downward often causing the chin wrinkle and become more prominent.

There are two concerns in Deception Management related to the emotion sadness:

1. If sadness is felt, but hidden or otherwise repressed, it is a deception meaning the subject does not want others to know what they are feeling. This is of concern if the subject might act on their sadness – such as a suicidal individual.

2. If an expression of sadness is being falsified, it is a deception where the subject is seeking to elicit something from others (sympathy, handouts, favors, etc.).

## Happiness (Smile)

A person's expression of happiness is usually thought of as a simple smile. However, fake smiles are often used to mask other emotions and frequently occur immediately following a micro expression of some other emotion.

A genuine smile occurs and disappears smoothly. However, the offset time of a false smile may seem noticeably inappropriate; dropping off too abruptly or decreasing in steps as the smile leaves the face. In large or broad smiles, the eyebrows may move down very slightly if at all. Real smiles include a tightening of the eyelids – producing crow's feet- but if the eyelid tightening is asymmetrical (unbalanced) it does not signal real enjoyment (it is probably a false smile). Generally, a false smile does not involve the muscles around the eyes.

If the smile lasts more than about 5 seconds, it is likely to be false, covering or masking another felt emotion. False smiles are sometimes used as a gestural emblem, providing a particular meaning to a situation according to the context of that situation. If the false smile is a mask for fear or distress, the reliable muscles in the forehead may still appear.

Many people confuse expressed contempt for a smile. The contempt (often called a 'smirk') appears as a one sided smile, but the enjoyment is the feeling of superiority, not generalized happiness. The chief difference between a contempt smile and a felt happiness smile is the one-sided tightened and raised lip corner.

In summary, false smiles are used to cover up other emotions or send specific signals other than happiness. False smiles do not lower the eyebrows or engage the circular muscles around the eyes which are partially associated with crow's feet (but not totally – so the presence of crow's feet alone is insufficient for concluding a smile is genuine happiness).

<u>Example of use</u>: At a meeting where a merger is being announced. The representative of the controlling company states, "Unfortunately, many layoffs are expected and we are very sorry for that." However, immediately upon stating "we are very sorry for that" the representative reveals a micro-expression indicating contempt or happiness; the "sorry" comment is unlikely to be the real feelings of the representative. Instead, the representative is feeling superior to the people being addressed or they are indicating they are happy at the prospect of people being laid off. In both situations, a determination of deception would be valid.

If on the other hand, the representative presented a micro or subtle expression suggesting sadness or depression, and their body language seems to be in agreement with those emotions, the representative is most likely being honest in the apology.

When people try to hide their true felt emotions, they are trying to deceive others of their present feelings. Combining this awareness with the information from other tactics can greatly enhance our understanding of the situation including, among other things, whether there is an effort to deceive.

## Summary and Conclusion

Because we have been studying faces since infancy, we have become pretty good at identifying the emotions expressed. At the same time, we have also learned to hide our emotions due to being aware of how exceptionally attentive people are at reading facial expressions. Most deception recognition programs generally avoid analyzing facial expressions, believing people place too much emphasis on controlling their face and its expressions, making it too difficult and unreliable to evaluate. However, this section's information will enhance the ability of the practitioner to discover the hidden emotions of the face and whether the person is being honest or deceptive.

In general, a determination of honesty or deception through expression/emotion analysis is a two stage process. In stage one, a determination of the true felt emotion must be made. Step two then compares the felt emotion to other communicated messages to determine whether the messages are in agreement or if they contradict one another.

Once an expression is identified, the determination of deception is based on whether the expression conflicts with other signals – especially body language, covering expressions, and word based contradictions.

When identified emotions conflict with other forms of communication (expressions, behaviors, or words) a determination of deception can be reached. If, however, the various forms of communication are in sync (they re-enforce one another and the felt emotion) the person is being honest in what they are communicating.

To be effective in this approach, the investigator must be highly observant, knowledgeable of the various forms of communication, and knowledgeable in determining whether those forms of communication re-enforce one another.

# 8 DISCOURSE ANALYSIS

## Introduction

Discourse Analysis is a process of extracting embedded information from communications by analyzing and comparing the contents. Discourse Analysis, a sub-discipline of linguistics, is also known as Content Analysis, Statement Content Analysis, and Criterion Based Content Analysis among others.

Discourse Analysis is focused on the structure, patterns and contents of verbal or textual communications and is concerned with verbal and written communications such as speeches, conversational exchanges and written communications. It is not used to consider, evaluate or analyze nonverbal or non-textual communications.

This method is based on research based conventions of social communication such as grammatical rules and structure, use of time and much more. These components of analysis are used because they remain consistent so that we can effectively communicate with one another.

Although Discourse Analysis can be used to reveal deception, it possesses the potential of revealing a great deal more depth in analysis than just the veracity of the content. In fact, using Discourse Analysis in conjunction with other deception management approaches can produce a startling amount of valid and usable information.

This approach is especially effective because most people are unaware of how much information is communicated as they subconsciously follow the guidelines of grammar, syntax, social convention and habitual practices.

Using Discourse Analysis to deconstruct our communications can reveal personal definitions, relationship information, time frames, deception indicators, psychological issues, attitudes, and much more.

Every sentence a person uses is constructed via an editing process. When experiencing something, you have a mental recording of virtually every detail. When you choose to relate an experience, you have to filter all the content you do not want to include and then construct what you want to communicate from what remains.

For example, when a respondent is asked what they did today before arriving at work they state: "I got up at 7 am. I exercised, got breakfast, dealt with the dog and after that, got my kids up and ready for school. After they left I got in the car and drove to work."

This communication did not include the unimportant or seemingly irrelevant things you did such as brushing your teeth, tying your shoes or what food was on the breakfast menu. However, the subject gave some clues to other things. He was aware of and included the exact time he got up. Otherwise he would have used a qualifier (I think I got up at 7 am) or a vagueness inducer (I got up pretty early). Since this was the only time mentioned, it suggests it was important enough to note, possibly because the alarm clock goes off at that time. He mentioned breakfast before getting the kids up, so he did not have breakfast with the kids.

He also mentioned that he, "dealt with the dog" which suggests that the dog had to be dealt with. Dealing with something often implies an unpleasant task. Possibly the dog had to be walked, fed or cleaned up after. Using "the dog" rather than the dog's name "Sam" or a possessive reference such as "my dog" suggests that at that moment, and possibly longer, he was not overly fond of the relationship; maybe because of the unpleasant task – could the dog have done something undesirable like having an accident on the carpet?

By referring to the kids as "MY" kids, he is using a personal possessive pronoun which implies that the kids are his responsibility (at least at that time) and he has a pretty good relationship with them (again at that time). From this it is easy to see how a breakdown of words and meanings can provide a vast amount of information that can be further investigated in an interview focused on revealing the details of the areas within the statement that the analyst believes may be useful.

There are positives and negatives to this approach. One particularly relevant positive and negative characteristic is that while Discourse Analysis requires extensive training to extract all the hidden information, an incredible amount is available with proper training. In that light, another potential negative is that the potential for such depth is based on theory and has not been strictly evaluated for validity at that level.

Although there is a vast amount of training needed to be able to extract great detail from a statement (if such is eventually proven valid), a survey of the major features, along with some practice, can provide an amazing amount of information from someone's communications.

However, Deception Management relies on multiple methods of analysis to increase validity of findings. As a result, it is recommended that a video or audio recording be obtained when possible. This allows for a record, verbatim, of what was said as well as all the indicators that are based on evaluations of visual and auditory behaviors.

The best information for analysis comes from unbiased sources of communication. Since anything and everything a person says can bias a statement, it is important to collect the statement or discourse contents before they have been externally contamination. This must always be of concern because contamination, even if it is the result of accidental and naïve actions, can bias what we include and what words we use to describe what is included. The following example illustrates how easy it is to contaminate someone's editing process changing how they might phrase the contents of their statement:

You are sent to investigate reports that John Doe abused his wife earlier in the week. The two following introductions provide opportunities for collecting different information as will be explained:

"Hello, my name is Jane Smith. I am working with the police department. I am investigating a call you made on Thursday that your husband physically abused you. I see by the mark on your face that there was an injury, so please tell me how he did that and why."

In her response she described that she had decided to drop the charges. Anyway, he came home from work already angry about her mother visiting and when she tried to talk with him, he fought with her and she was hit in face. The investigator, based on this response had the husband arrested (an arrest in such circumstances is required by law in many areas when there is an injury from domestic abuse).

In this second introduction, the information is slightly different, but the differences allow for a better determination of what really went on and produces a different outcome.

"Hello, my name is Jane Smith. I was sent to follow up on a call you made to the police on Thursday. Can you tell me what happened? Please be thorough. I need to know every detail you can think of so that I get a clear picture."

In response to this question, she stated that the situation resulted from days of arguing about her mother coming for a visit. On Wednesday she told him that her mother was coming and that was that. This led to an argument in which he got angry and left and did not return until after work on Thursday. When he got home he was in a bad mood because the mother was already there, even though she wasn't supposed to come until the weekend. He got mad and went to the bedroom and packed his clothes to leave until the mother left. The wife came in to tell him how unreasonable he was and when she saw him packing she grabbed the clothes out of the suitcase. He tried to grab them from her and as she was yanking on a plastic clothes hanger, it snagged on the suitcase hitting her in the face. She got angry and told him to just get the hell out. When he left, her mother insisted that the mark was the result of his abuse and insisted that she report it since there was no harm in being too careful.

As is obvious, the second approach which reduced limitations and eliminated bias presented the potential that the call was the result of an accident that occurred and there was no actual abuse from the husband and no arrest was called for.

In theory, the best approach is to simply ask "What happened?" However, while this will get the most unbiased of data, it is not very practical in many instances. If at all possible, allow the subject (the statement's author) to determine everything they include such as when and where the statement should begin, end and what it should contain.

If they ask – where do you want me to start, you respond with "Wherever you think is important." and apply this approach to all questions.

Once you have the statement, you can move into analyzing it. What do you analyze and how? The analysis components include the overall balance of events, added, missing and irrelevant information, use of introductions, titles and parts of speech, where emphasis was placed and where the events start and stop. Each of these is described along with the analysis criteria in the following sections.

An important aspect of statement analysis is that relationship quality and emotions often change throughout the statement in accordance to the events occurring at that same point in the statement. Also, for evaluation purposes, consider the statement as being composed of mini chapters or sub-events – each taking up space within the overall statement.

# Component Analysis

Many of the descriptions are based on analysis of written statements. If you are working with 'live' or recorded sources of information, you will need to make adjustments as best you can determine for the unique circumstance of each situation.

## Event Statement Balance

**Event Statement Balance** is a comparison of the content ratios between the parts of a statement. Every statement is a description of things that have already happened. This means that in most statements the entire event took place in the past. As a result, when a person gives their story (the statement) they typically include three basic sections:
1. Before (often called the prologue) - What happened before the main event.
2. During – A description of the main event.
3. After (often called the epilogue) - What happened after the main event.

By comparing the relative amount of content of each section, a rough determination can be established about statement balance. If reviewing a recorded statement (written, audio or video) you can literally measure the different sections by counting the number of lines (if written) or by timing the various sections if audio or video.

To use this aspect of analysis, identify and distinguish each component by some identifiable demarcation (a line, a note added in, etc.). This gives an estimate of their relative proportions. Although this is usually sufficient, a more accurate evaluation can be made by counting the words of each section and dividing that by the total number of words. This gives an exact relative amount of coverage of each section.

If you are interacting in real time, you have to make an 'on the spot guess' about the relative balance of the sections.

Normally, in a true statement, the 'Before' and 'After' components are roughly equal in content while the "during" section contains the bulk of the contents.

The 'Before' section usually contains an introduction to the situation, an introduction to the actors within the event and a description of the circumstances prior to the main event. This section tends to be the largest section in false statements. The presumption is that a long introduction allows the subject to delay addressing the main event because it is something they would prefer to avoid.

The 'During' section describes the main event. It frequently contains fragments of unrelated material that come to mind while recalling the situation or as part of their description of what they were thinking as it was occurring. This section is proportionally largest section in statements that are honest.

The 'After' section usually describes what occurs following the main event. If the event were highly emotional (such as in a violent event like a fight, rape or robbery) the 'after' section normally contains significant amounts of emotional content that express the impact in personal terms, after effects on their life, fears about the future and so on. A lack of content in the 'after' section is either a person who is very detailed (fact oriented), provided the statement in a list format (like a shopping list) instead of an 'essay format' or they were not being honest and the emotional impact is not there because it did not happen.

Generally, in an honest recollection, a rough bell curve of content is what you should be looking for. If the statement is written, the amount of page space (or lines on a page) can be measured. In a live interview where measurement may not be possible focus on the time it takes for the person to get to the main point and the length of the 'after' section and estimate whether there is balance and emotion. Beware of those that present lots of details but avoid personal sensory descriptions, don't recite what others said as they said them, or just abruptly end.

Although Discourse Analysis can be used effectively with the above guidelines, the detailed research findings that follow will significantly increase conclusion accuracy:

## Research Findings in Statement Honesty and Deception

### Focus on Honesty:

1. When the proportion of words found in the 'after' section is greater than the 'before' section, the statement is likely truthful.
2. Truthful statements tend to have 'after' sections that include descriptions of their emotions (fear, anger, embarrassment or shock) especially in serious crimes and severe events.
3. Truthful statements contain more exact quotes when describing what was said.
4. Truthful statements contain less visual information, but significantly more auditory, temporal and affective (emotionally oriented) information.
5. Truthful statements tend to have more unique sensory details overall and most especially in the 'during' section. Note: The absence of sensory details, especially when combined with a relatively short 'during' section identifies areas to focus on in follow-up interviews.
6. Honest experiences include more affective information such as emotional reactions than do created events. Victims and witnesses of quickly occurring traumatic events may not notice their emotions until the trauma ended. Emotional observations are more likely to appear in the 'after' section of a statement. As the severity of the event increases so does the inclusion of emotional descriptors.

**Focus on Deception:**

1. Deceptive statements (oral and written) include more negatives throughout and especially in the 'before' section. Negatives are anything with 'no' or 'not' or any contractions of those.
2. Deceptive oral statements include more repeating of words and phrases.
3. Deceptive oral statement authors make less eye contact when they believe it is very important their deception be believed.
4. The use of qualifiers (safe-outs or escape phrases) are strongly associated with deception especially when found in the 'before' section. Note: There are three varieties of safe outs: Uncertainty expressions (I'm not sure but…). Weakening modifiers (kind of, sort of…) and Vague phrases (something like …).
5. The greater the presence of unique sensory details, the greater the likelihood of honesty. Unique sensory details include specific descriptions of perceptions (auditory, visual, kinesthetic, gustatory, or olfactory) without the inclusion of qualifiers (safe-outs). Also many deceptive people try to emulate honesty by including a lot of non-sensory but factual details ("I saw four tires on one car burning and at least three people were running around screaming") as opposed to sensory and emotive feelings ("The stench from the burning tires made me feel sick to my stomach and the people were screaming "help me, help me").
6. Note: This is not true if they exist primarily or only in the 'before' section. An introduction filled with sensory details followed by the 'during' section lacking them, suggests deception and a follow up focused interview about critical details should follow. Although the presence of sensory details indicates an increased likelihood that the detailed part of the statement is truthful, the other sections of the statement may be deceptive or completely false. Examples: Honest statement: "I could tell the house was burning because of the flickering lights I could see through the windows. I knew it was bad as soon as smelled the rubber tires on the cars in the garage burning." Deceptive statement: "I could tell the house was on fire because of the flames in the windows. The cars in the garage even caught fire."

## Content Use of Time and Space

A second component is the use of time and space throughout the statement. The goal is to identify aspects of a statement that contain much more or much less content than other parts. Once those are identified, determine if the amount of content makes sense. In short, where and what is the content focused on? Similarly, in content sections that contain little information, is there a reason for the lack of content?

For evaluation purposes, look at the statement as a series of mini chapters or sub-events – each taking up space within the overall statement. Since they can never give every detail, they must edit the content within each chapter. For analysis purposes we must fall back on the Law of Human Behavior "Everything we do, we do for a reason" by asking ourselves, "Why did they edit the information the way they did?"

When what should be a significant event is included but seems to have elicited little interest and makes up very little of the content, it should be considered a potentially important and concerning piece of information. Why is there not more detail and focus on that important event? Alternately, a minor aspect (that is over estimated) of a larger event means that it is very important to the subject. Again, the question is why? Why is an insignificant detail being focused on so much that it takes up an abnormal share of the statement considering what it seems to be?

# Unexpected, Inappropriate and Absent Information

## Introduction

When asked to construct a statement about an experienced event, we communicate our view of what transpired. Because we cannot (nor would we want to) incorporate every detail of an event, we edit the content of our experiences so that our statement includes what we consider to be relevant information. We also filter out or minimize trivial and seemingly unimportant information so that the information we provide conforms to our perceptions, considerations and goals (conscious and subconscious).

Even when we provide what we believe to be the honest truth, we may add information that may seem irrelevant and we may leave out relevant information without realizing it. Similarly, when we want to deceive, we may add, minimize or remove pertinent information in our effort to misinform.

## Added Content

Added content is information that seems as though it is unrelated, unimportant or irrelevant in the effort to communicate the relevant and significant facts concerning an event. However, to the person who chose to add that information even though it was seemingly meaninglessness, to them it was included for some important reason. If it were truly unimportant and irrelevant, it would have been filtered out. When a statement includes this type of added information we need to determine why these seemingly insignificant details were included.

For instance, while at work the police contact you and ask you to recount your morning because a neighbor's parked car was vandalized. In the description you include details about brushing your teeth. That sub-event seems rather insignificant and irrelevant. However, if your bathroom sink began flooding while brushing your teeth, the relevance to you is clear. Although this has nothing to do with their vandalized car, that event is of significance to you and is on your mind when recalling the morning events.

When honest information is added, but unrelated to the event, it is often about things on the subject's mind and is usually described in emotional terms. They tend to express the verbal as they accompany it with nonverbal gestures and other non-verbal communications (using illustrators and gestures that seem to be coordinated to their demeanor).

They will also tend to accompany the physical actions through gestures that help re-enact aspects of the event. The re-enacting would include actions such their eyes looking the direction indicated by the statement or a gestures of things actually performed. Another aspect of honest statements is the inclusion of details that are objectively verifiable.

If, however, you obtain what seems unnecessarily added information but can find no clear reason for its inclusion, it is a likely effort to be deceptive as 'added detail for believability'.

Research shows that it is common for the deceptive to imply honesty by including additional details in their statement. As covered in "Statement Balance", if unnecessary information is added to the 'Before' section of an event statement it may indicate an avoidance of the main issue.

## Missing Content
Understated or Skipped Over 'Important' Content

When we identify a segment (sub-chapter) we believe is significant but the provided information has little relevant content, it is either because the information is truly unimportant or the information has unstated content that is significant but withheld.

If the material is actually trivial, such as putting on one's socks or when they fail to provide details of a long and uneventful road trip, an unambiguous and simple explanation is usually offered immediately if asked.

On the other hand, people also minimize or edit out very important content if they are fearful it might reveal things they do not want known due to reasons such as guilt or embarrassment; even if the information is not relevant to the situation under consideration.

Identifying Missing Content
There are recognizable signs when a segment is not trivial:
1. They mention clearly relevant events but fail to elaborate.
2. They use skip words or phrases (bridges) to bypass details.
3. They skip over significant amounts of time.

Text-Bridges
When these occur they are often preceded with tell-tale indicators known as text-bridges. Text-bridges, which research has found to be reliable indicators of missing information, are efforts to shift from one topic to another through the use of commonly used words or phrases.

Although many different words or phrases may be used, research has found that the following words account for over 90% of such efforts (in order of frequency): 'Then', 'So', 'After', 'When', 'As', 'While', and 'Next'.

Minimized versus Bridged Content
Example of minimized content: When asking how a friend's fantasy vacation was, you receive the comment, "Oh, I had a pretty good time." The lack of detail and the use of "pretty" as a qualifier in "Pretty Good" both indicate deception. Based solely on this response, a reasonable conclusion would be that the vacation was less successful than expected and the friend is reluctant to discuss it.

Example of bridged content: When a person claiming to be the victim of robbery is asked what happened he replies, "I was walking down 48$^{th}$ street looking at the window displays, then I felt a gun in my back and a heard some guy tell me not to turn around . . .". Although this sentence has several deception indicators, the use of the skip term (the bridge) "then" indicates a bridge that probably has more detailed content if elaborated on.

Obtaining Skipped Information
Begin asking for details at the point just prior to the first text bridge (such as the physical orientation of those involved, what others ordered for dinner, what happened before you got into the car, etc.) and then ask what happened next.

If it seems that requesting more information at that point detracts from the interviewing process, explanations or apologies may help retain rapport while keeping the process moving forward.

Examples include remarks, such as "I'm sorry. I think I missed something"; "Can you clarify something for me," or "I am sure my boss will ask me what happened at . . . can you elaborate on that for me?", etc. Although honest people may become irritated with the process, a simple apology should quell the irritation and their relating of facts will continue.

The interview will fill in details until another text bridge is used to span the now shrinking gap and the concerning information will become harder to disguise. Continue by repeating the same process starting at just before the second text bridge and so forth until all time and action is accounted for.

As the gap closes, this systematic narrowing of the information gap is like a psychological vise increasing the stress which is identifiable by autonomic nervous system activation (physiological changes that are difficult to control).

Eventually, the information gap becomes so small that the subject can no longer find words to bridge the gap, their efforts to avoid that content become very obvious or they try a completely different tactic such as false anger.

## Things Not Done

When comments of things "not done" are mentioned, they are often important to the statement's author; otherwise they would not mention them at all. For example, stating, "We didn't cry", indicates the importance of that fact and suggests that crying was a realistic option and not doing so is of significance to that person.

## Names and Titles

In a statement where people are mentioned, how names and titles are used provide a description of the type and character of the relationship. When a person (or sometimes even a pet) is introduced, the introduction normally includes their name (who is referred to) AND their relative title (their role, status, or relationship).

When first introduced, if both name AND title are not given, it is likely that there is a relationship problem between the person introduced and the person introducing them.

As the statement continues, it is normal to refer to the person by either name OR title. However, if a different title or name is later substituted; this indicates a change in how that person is viewed by the author.

Examples:
Good relationship: "John this is Mr. Turner, our company CEO".
Poor Relationship: "John this is Mr. Turner".

When introducing his wife to friends, a man states, "This is Donna, my wife." Later when he is asked to join them for a boy's night out at the local bar he replies, "I would really like to, but you know the 'old ball and chain' would frown on it." This change of title – from 'wife' to 'old ball and chain' - indicates the interpersonal relationship the man and wife have concerning going to the bar with the guys.

When indications suggest that a relationship has changed, events in the statement often give clues as to why the change took place; Such as in reference to going with the guys to the bar.

In a follow-up interview, focusing on the events that took place just prior to the change often reveals the cause of the title change and may describe the character of the associated relationship.

## Nouns

Nouns are references to "things" with each having its own definition. When people choose the words they are going to use, they select them based on how they define them. When they swap one word for another, they also swap one definition for another. Similar words are just that, "similar". Minor differences of definition are often significant because we tend to carefully define the nouns we use.

If "crazy" is later changed to "eccentric" the difference in meaning is considerable. When a noun has been used in one part of a statement and then the subject later uses a similar different noun referring to the same 'thing' the change in how they define the thing may have been changed to mislead others with the idea that they will consider the slight change as insignificant, when their change is very significant to what is being said. Again this is similar to deceiving through editing.

Example: Cindy's mother restricted Cindy from going to the mall. One of Cindy's friends called to ask if she would go shopping with her at the mall. Since Cindy knows that her mom thinks of the mall as a shopping complex of many stores with a common pedestrian area, she announces to her mother, "Mom, I'm going to the store with Lisa. I'll be back soon." By using "store" in place of mall, she implies a singular shop, not the mall. But the mother hearing 'store' does not think Cindy is thinking 'mall' and allows her to go.

## Pronouns

Pronouns are words that substitute for nouns. The most common pronouns: I, you, he, she, we, they, my, his, her, ours, me, us, him, them, myself, and ourselves; each infer measures of relationships to those included in the pronoun.

People use pronouns frequently without realizing how precise the inherent meanings are. Similarly, they tend to not notice how others use pronouns and in fact have a tendency to overlook them unless they make a point of it, as in this training approach.

When interacting, people use pronouns to describe relationships in the past or present. In descriptions of past events, pronouns normally describe the quality of the relationship as it was at that time. Pronouns referring to present or future situations describe the relationship in the present or as they presently hope will be.

Possessive pronouns have specific usefulness in identifying the quality of relationship. To most people, "I" is the single most important word. Failure to use the "I" in singular references shows a lack of personal dedication to what is said. A statement made by an individual about themselves singularly without "I" suggests a lack of confidence in what was said (a likely deception).

How people use personal pronouns is also revealing. Like "I", "my" is very personally important. Use of "my" indicates a personal responsibility to the subject matter. For instance stating "my bills" instead of "our bills" suggests a personal responsibility for those bills.

Finally, when using the personal pronoun, "I", we place ourselves in the statement. When an "I" is expected but not present, there is a lack of commitment to what was said - a strong indicator of deception unless this is a consistent pattern for this person.

Similarly, in group references (we, they, you and I, etc.), "we" is the pronoun with the closest possible connections to others. Using "I" with other pronouns that describes a situation with others is a way to separate the statement author from the others mentioned. This distancing indicates the subject sees themselves as more important than the others mentioned.

The further apart the subject places "I" from the other referenced people in the sentence, the weaker the relationship.

The weakest reference is when you objectify the others with a word such as "with" where the "I" is on one side of the sentence and "with" in the middle and where the other pronouns are on the opposite side.

In a statement, changes of pronoun usage may indicate changes that were occurring in the relationship as the events unfolded. It is important to note that changes in pronouns usually occur just before significant events. Identifying changes may identify pivotal events.

## Verbs

Verbs indicate and describe action. Like nouns, they often possess unique definitions, subtle meanings and underlying innuendo. For example – Talking, Discussing, and Sharing each convey information between people; yet talking is communicating with little emotion (We were just talking); discussing suggests a more serious topic with opposing views (We were discussing how to punish Johnny); Sharing suggests a commonly accepted and more personal interaction (We're sharing ideas).

Generally when we speak of past events, they use past tense, present events use present tense, and future events use future tense.

While many deception training programs presume that violating this tendency means deception, psychological studies repeatedly show that people often mentally re-live a past event when recalling it. In doing so, they may use present tense verbs. The same is likely to also be true for imagining future events.

In both cases, placing themselves in the moment is communicated as though the "out of time" event were in the present. This means that the use of present tense may just as likely be non-deceptive as it is deceptive.

# Summary/Conclusion

When analyzing a person's statement, a great deal of hidden information can be identified. Information can reveal deception outright, additional details worthy of follow-up investigation such as, relative states of relationships, changes in those relationships, and much more depending on the content of the communication being analyzed.

# 9 COMPARATIVE ANALYSIS

Each method of analysis (reflex, response, conscious choice, emotional expression and discourse analysis) possesses unique indicators of honesty and deception. While any one method can produce accurate evaluations of deception above chance, the best single method accuracy rate is still only about 70%.

Much greater levels of effectiveness can be achieved if multiple methods are used in concert with each serving to complement the others and to support a cross verification of consistency or inconsistency. When an inconsistency is identified between various methods of analysis or channels of communication it most probably represents a valid (correct) and reliable (consistent) indicator of deception. In other words, deception is implied anytime there is a conflict between co-existing signals from the different analysis methods. The greater number of signals someone is able to observe, the greater chance of catching inconsistencies (deception).

True, felt emotions are expressed unconsciously and can be categorized according to the emotion felt. A contradiction between an expression and another mode of communication indicates deception. In this event, the expression should be considered representative of the actual felt emotions.

Contradictions include expressions that indicate an emotion the verbal message does not support. While the contradiction may be between expressed emotion and other forms of communication (including writing and overt body language) the primary deception recognition comes from expression and discourse (verbal and written communication); for instance, a comment that is not supported by an expression.

Although ideally a more solid determination would result if the expression, the discourse and gestures are in disagreement with one another.

When people are honest, the components of their behavioral system communicate in coordination with one another when presenting information that agrees with a felt expression - the words and actions match. Since this agreement between systems is a natural manner of behaving, it requires practically no higher thought or conscious concern.

Signal inconsistency refers to a mismatch of communicated information that has been provided between the different communication systems. Dishonesty usually involves people consciously trying to coordinate all their forms of communication in an effort to appear 'honest'. However, since there are many ways people communicate, there are many opportunities for mismatches to occur. While many of these can be controlled with some effort, keeping track of all of them at once is very difficult. This is why some actors are excellent liars; they are highly practiced at controlling all their messages in order to convince the audience of the reality of their stage character.

On the other hand, some forms of communicating are virtually uncontrollable and most people cannot disguise them such as the following: pupil dilation, facial flushing, facial muscle movements, micro-expressions and subtle expressions.

Unconscious Reflex actions are primarily unconscious behaviors resulting from stress. When an autonomic nervous system indicator conflict (message reflex) is present, stress is present. By careful observation or interaction, the source of the stress may be identified.

However, the mere presence of stress does not mean deception. For example, behaving nervously has many causes including fear, anger, guilt, and certain memories as well as the nervousness from deceiving. The source can be determined by identifying related behavioral clusters if the specific stressing topic is brought up at a later time.

Unlike unconscious reflexes, people can control their subconscious behaviors once they become consciously aware of them. These include body language, gestures, illustrators, and manipulators as well as the overall words and sentence and grammatical structure of what is said.

Because these behaviors are normally under subconscious control, their presentations tend to be involuntary – something like driving a car. Once people become accustom to driving, they give little thought to the minor variations made in steering as they drive along on a highway, but when the need arises they have the ability to take complete conscious control. For that reason, subconscious behaviors are many times more involved and subtle than those involved in driving, when people try to control them they often do so with actions that do not seem fluid or well timed (jerky, clumsy or unnatural).

When a conscious statement is made, the subconscious behaviors will either support the statement or they won't. Their lack of support can be seen in unmatched signals (such as kinesic leaks) indicating deception. If people are trying to take conscious control so that these behaviors reflect what they are saying, the effort to control these will come across as jerky and unnatural, again deceptive.

For example when using their hands to describe something, if the hand illustrations do not match (or they may directly conflict) with the verbal descriptions, the message is in disagreement. However, because people gain conscious control over these behaviors, the mismatch is often rapidly corrected so that the message becomes in agreement with the statement.

Conscious Behaviors are the most controllable of all indicators. If a contradiction is identified between a conscious behavior and any of the other means of communication, or indicator systems, deception is occurring although the cause for the deception may be unclear.

The primary conscious behavior for comparison purposes are verbal statements and their associated meaning. Additionally, an effort to mask an expression is clearly a conscious act and should be evaluated for comparison with other signals.

Using Discourse Analysis as indicated earlier (our use of words and grammar) may also show discord with other signals again suggesting deception. However, without extensive material for comparisons, individual variations can easily account for the apparent conflicts. Most often these communication conflicts are valid indications of deceit and the investigator should determine if additional indicators are present. If they are, they greatly support and strengthen a determination of deception.

# Deception Identification Summary

Each approach to deception identification addresses one of the four basic components of deception: motivation and decision, deception construction, communicating deception and the deception as a product of the communication. Each component possesses characteristic and clues that can be used to manage the potential or actual deception.

## Motivation and Decision

Human deception is always purposeful and is generally fear based. The stimulus is either a desire for, or an avoidance of, something specific. Management consists of techniques to inhibit deception (Inhibiting Deception/Eliciting honesty) primarily by altering their motivation and the resulting decisions so that deception is no longer considered as a good option. Note: if the subject possibly has the motivation and feels they must provide an immediate response to a concerning question, they may simply lie. This can be managed through Comparative and Expression Analysis.

## Construction

Once deception is seriously considered, the subject must go through the mental effort to develop a deception. This process can be identified by identifying out of place or inappropriate accessing of the internal dialogue or through stalling efforts (to gain additional thinking time).

## Communication Process

When individuals deceive they must transmit the deception effort to others. This effort can be identified by the way the person communicates, emotional analysis and comparative behavioral analysis.

## The Product

When individuals deceive they create a statement that communicates the deception. This product can be identified and analyzed with the techniques of Discourse Analysis.

# Conclusion

With each stage in deceiving covered with one or more identification techniques, the trained investigator has multiple opportunities to identify, refine and manage deception when it occurs.

Although the fundamentals of each deception identification method have been revealed, practice is necessary to enhance the learned skills. For those with specialized and highly specific needs, advanced training in each area is recommended.

# Section 3

## OBTAINING INFORMATION
### Eliciting Honesty/Inhibiting Deception

Ultimately Deception Management is about collecting information from others. While we gain a great deal of information through pure observation (such as through body language) the greatest specificity, detail, depth and quality of content is provided through our intentional verbally based communications.

The most effective and efficient way to obtain the information possessed by others this is through the interview process with the application of careful interviewing practices. Interviewing is a science of interpersonal persuasion, logic, psychology and cultural understanding.

# 10 INTERVIEWING

The term interview as used refers to the interactional give and take between people in an effort to obtain information. This encompasses a variety of ways we gain information; ranging from innocuous information gathering such as talking with friends in order to find out something desired (simple information collecting), to formal interviewing which may have a more significant personal impact (such as a job interview) to a police interview where an investigation uses the interview to collect facts. Most intense is the interview process referred to as the interrogation which is often for the sole purpose to manipulate and coerce.

## Rules and Guidelines of Interviewing

### Rule #1
### *One to One Interaction*

One to one interaction: The presence of others complicates interpersonal dynamics and reduces rapport development. However, if overwhelming intimidation is desired (i.e. good cop and bad cop) multiple interviewers may be useful.

### Rule #2
### *The Interview Starts Before You Know It*

From the subject's perspective, when the situation is a formal interview, the interview began as soon as the subject becomes aware of your role as the interviewer.

## Rule #3
## *Get Uncontaminated Statement*

In a situation where a statement is useful, it is necessary to obtain the statement before it has been biased or contaminated any more than necessary. Every interaction prior to statement collection biases the statement. Collect a statement before you provide any information or interact beyond what is absolutely necessary.

## Rule #4
## *They Know More Than They Realize*

Always "assume more data is available!" When people relate anything they experience, they always filter out a great deal of information. What is filtered may be significant.

# Interview Preparations

## Preparing the Interviewer Emotionally

In criminal and psychological interviews, it is likely that events of great horror are sometimes discussed and are often discussed in detail. To keep the cooperation of the interviewee, the interviewer must not give any hint they are making moral judgments. Indications that you are making such evaluations will often shut down interviewee cooperation, effectively ending the interview. However, to keep mentally healthy we must prepare ourselves to avoid swallowing the monster (as phrased by Sigmund Freud). This is done by providing some form for emotional venting since such horrendous events are emotionally disturbing. Generally speaking the use of a professional counselor is the best course of action.

## Environmental Preparations (Setting the Stage)

If the situation is a formal interview; properly setting the stage can be of great influence and doing so means taking into account several considerations and options. These include: where to meet, location layout, seating arrangements, décor, and distractions.

## Place and Space

When people meet, especially if there is a potential for deception, properly setting the stage may be very important. The more empowered a person feels, the easier it is for them to choose deception and they will provide fewer fear indicators.

It is usually intimidating to conduct an interview in an institutional setting such as a police station or security office. Intimidation can result in false readings. Reduce intimidation by removing symbols of authority and making the setting as neutral as possible.

When an interview must take place at the subject's work location, arrange for a nearby area or room where work activities produce a minimum of distractions.

If you interview a subject in his or her home, keep in mind that they will feel more empowered there and that makes it easier for them to be less cooperative and more deceitful. SO if the home is the location where you must interview conduct the interview in a room that is as neutral as possible.

Normally, when a person is in their home, they will try to arrange the interview to take place in their comfort zone (their power spot); Allowing them to do so increases their confidence and their sense of empowerment promoting resistance to sensitive questions.

If the interview is to be conducted in the home and they have seemingly selected a room that is probably their comfort zone, find an excuse to move to another area. You can offer comments or questions such as, "I think that we might have less interference in the kitchen" or "the dining room chairs would help my bad back, can we move into there?" These requests for assistance may also establish or re-enforce rapport while also helping to equalize the sense of power. Always remember that the saying "A man's home is his castle" is not only true, it also applies to women. Major exceptions are if the subject is a victim or a young child. In these situations the added comfort may increase their sense of security.

Example: You are in a client's home. They take their power chair (the recliner) and they direct you to sit on a couch that is lower and clearly at a disadvantage. You notice a kitchen table with straight-back chairs. Suggest that you move to the kitchen as the chairs will provide better support for you aching back.

# Room Environment

The environment of a room influences the behaviors and attitudes of the people within it. If you can select the room, the ideal situation would be an area not too small or too large; usually about 10 feet by 10 feet. Make sure the room is generally comfortable (lighting, temperature, smells, etc.). During an interview, the door should be closed, but access to it should not appear as being closed off. Furnishings should include chairs with a desk for paperwork that does not interfere with observing the behaviors of the subject or serve as a physical barrier. Try to arrange seating where you have the best opportunity for observing the interviewee as innocently as possible. Although the reason has not been securely identified, studies show a significant improvement in discerning deception when the left ear is closest to the source (the interviewee).

At the beginning of the interview, it is best to have the chairs at a conversational distance of about 6 feet apart. This provides the best comfort range for the typical American in the company of others with who they are somewhat unfamiliar. Starting out too close will increase stress and tension masking important responses when evaluating behavioral reactions. If you are too far apart you produce a perception of being in the 'hot-seat'.

In general, the fewer distractions you can provide, the better you will be in reading the subjects nonverbal communications. Distracting items (ornaments, clutter, etc.), situations (temperature, lighting, smells, etc.) and events (ringing telephones, TVs, conversations, noisy machines, etc.) all will reduce the ability to effectively evaluate behavior or determine behavioral indicators. Anything that can be a distraction can significantly interfere with your observation efforts.

As the interview progresses and rapport is established, the distance can be reduced to about four feet apart. While there are no exact rules, the interviewer must be attentive to the body language of the subject. If the subject feels threatened, rapport will be lost.

There are two causes of rapport loss due to proxemics: being too close and due to a perception of aggressiveness by closing the distance too quickly.

One tactic is to lean in as the interview continues. This allows you to gauge their response. If positive, lean back as you pull the chair under you forward. This gives the impression that you are not moving inward even though you have reduced the distance.

Generally, it is best to be as close as possible without evoking any kind of defense response. The closer you sit (without stressing the subject), the more comfortable they will be in sharing personal and sensitive information. Keep in mind that when two people of different sexes interact, distance may falsely communicate ulterior sexist motives. In these situations you MUST be sure to not intrude into the other person's space. Doing so may be interpreted as harassment or intimidation among other possible perceptions.

Another environmental issue concerns the existence of habitual behaviors. As previously discussed smoking, snacking, or other habitual behaviors should be discouraged since they serve as distractions that can contaminate the situation. However, if the need for cooperation is more important, allowing such behaviors may be effectively converted into something useful. If habitual behaviors cannot be eliminated, identify the behavior and their associated habitual patterns and use these as additional baseline measures.

# 11 ANTI-DECEPTION INTERVIEWING

When asking questions, how you ask them, what you ask, and the order in which the questions are presented dictate the quality of information you obtain.

## Requesting Assistance

When beginning an interview, several positive results may be achieved simply by asking the subject for assistance. Unless the subject is firmly fixed on not cooperating, this request can produce positive results. As a general rule, making such a request enhances rapport. It insinuates that you are on the same side, working together toward a common goal.

Requesting assistance invokes the social expectation that when you do someone a favor, they 'owe you one'. This is so well accepted that we have a host of common phrases reflecting that belief: "one good turn deserves another", "Scratch my back and I'll scratch yours", "tit for tat" and "quid pro quo". All of these indicate the power and influence of this tactic.

Another very effective approach is to give the impression the subject knows more than you. By asking for their help you allow them to think that they are more intelligent than you. This serves many purposes such as improving rapport, making them feel good about themselves, allowing the subject feel that they are a part of the situation rather than a mere subject within it, and it often results in them dropping their intellectual guard without concern.

This often results in the subject committing minor slip ups in their interaction. This approach was often used by and associated with the seemingly inept television character, police Lieutenant Columbo. By leading others to believe he was less intelligent and capable than he actually was, he was able to catch slip ups on many occasions. While this was a television show, many professional interviewers emulate this approach due to its success rate. However, if you overplay the role, it will be obvious and you will lose cooperation and rapport.

If you are requesting assistance from a victim or a victim's associates you are expecting them to mentally review a very unpleasant event in the hopes of obtaining useful information. In this situation the request must be sincere and the interview (or the question) should begin with a sincere apology for not only having to bother them, but in asking that they review such disturbing events.

# Questioning

## Rules of Questioning

When asking questions, following a few simple rules will improve the quality of answers.

### Clear and Simple Questions

When you ask a question make sure it is worded clearly and in a concise manner. This increases the chances that the response will also be clear and concise. If it is not, then it may be due to indicators meriting further probing. When a question is asked appropriately, the response can provide a great deal of useful information. If the question is unclear, the response will also be unclear and you will not know whether it is that way because of deception or due to a simple misunderstanding.

For example, wanting to know how long you have lived at your present address can be confusing if not worded properly. If I ask, "What is your present length of residence?" A response could be, "My house is 45 feet long." Since the goal was to establish the length of time at the present residence a better question would have been, "How many years have you lived at your present address?"

## One Question at a Time - (Do not Combine Questions)

When you ask a question, make sure you are only asking one thing at a time and that what you are asking is what you wish to learn. Questions that contain more than one issue can result in confused or deceptive responses and again the deception is masked; in this case due to the merging of the information that was requested.

For example, don't ask, "Tell me how and why you lost your last job and what you have been doing since." This assumes you LOST your last job. It also suggests a negative spin on the question increasing the stress. This question is actually asking several questions, each that could potentially lead to a greater quantity of pertinent information if asked properly.

How should these be asked? These are many possible ways to approach this same set of concerns and keep things neutral while also generating greater amounts of relevant information: Utilizing already produced information you have what is believed to be the last place the subject was employed. For that you can proceed with – "Why did you leave your last employed position", "What were the circumstances when you left", "If we contact that employer will they provide us with this same explanation" and so on. Then you can follow with a number of possibilities: "Have you been employed at all since that job", "If you have been employed, with whom" "When were you hired", "Why did you leave that employment", "If you have not been employed, (and time has passed or there is a lapse in time between listed jobs) what were you doing in that period of time?"

Note: in this case, using the term 'job' may be risky. A job is thought of as a place you work to earn money but tends to be separate from the concept of a career. Since both are employed positions, using employment is the better option.

Each of the previous questions is a potential fountain of useful information if evaluating an employment applicant. If indicators of concern are identified, they can be easily tied to a particular sub topic and pursued.

## Order Questions by Sensitivity

**Question sensitivity** refers to the mental discomfort felt when a person is asked a question he or she believes has a potential for being personally threatening. The greater the believed threat, the greater the sensitivity of the question.

Different situations may cause a non-threatening question to become threatening (more sensitive). For example: in a conversation with a friend about jobs, if you innocently asked; "How much do you make?" you probably would feel little concern (low sensitivity). However, if you have just asked the father of your girlfriend for his OK to marry his daughter, and he asks "how much do you make?" your perception would be that there is reason for concern (sensitivity) associated with your answer.

Keep in mind that the level of sensitivity is based on the situation and the subject's concern over the specific question.

Arrange topics and questions from least concerning to most concerning. Introducing highly sensitive questions can produce an emotional shock. This emotional reaction may have nothing to do with their response but the shock may result in flawed or misleading indicators.

With the exception of asking things to determine the shock value of the topic, the best approach is to ask questions in an increasing order of sensitivity. Asking low sensitivity questions first and then moving to questions of increasing sensitivity as the interview moves forward allows the subject to adjust so that indicators at each level of sensitivity are more recognizable and valid. By arranging the questions according to sensitivity, the subject's level of comfort can be improved with a resulting increase in the potential for obtaining honest responses.

Although you cannot know the sensitivity of every question, you can make educated guesses based on your knowledge of the person, circumstances, and general situational dynamics.

Ordering the questions from low to high sensitivity is similar to adding hot water bit by bit to a warm bath to make it hot. The goal is to start where the subject is comfortable and bit by bit introduce more sensitive questions. As the comfort level increases through familiarity and rapport building, the level of discomfort from the sensitive questions is lowered. In the end you are in very hot water, but it feels comfortable even though it was well beyond the previous comfort level.

In summary, begin with questions of little personal concern and as they become familiar with your style of questions, your voice, the room setting and so forth, they will become more comfortable with the questions as you ask them. As they become more comfortable, you can ask more sensitive questions without significantly increasing stress, resistance, and deception.

## Avoid Emotionally Charged Words

Avoid using words that have emotion invoking inferences. Using words that evoke emotion cause emotional and stress tainted responses due to the words used and not necessarily due to the response (considered or given).

A nurse trying to find out what drugs a patient has in their system before going in for surgery might not get an honest answer by asking, "What illegal drugs have you used recently?"

The phrase "illegal drugs" carries a lot of legal and emotional content. If the nurse asked, "What recreational substances have you used in the last 72 hours?" the answer may be more honest since 'recreational' does not imply violating the law nearly as directly as does the term 'illegal'.

## Allow Time For Responses

Do not rush the respondent to provide an answer. The process of considering the answer is often the main source of deception indicators.

Rushing an answer will more likely produce inaccurate responses and if deception is likely, cause an outright lie that in many cases is more difficult to identify. Allow time for the interviewee to think.

## Keep Your Eyes On The Subject

Many clues of deception can be missed if the interviewer is not very attentive and observant. Pay close attention to the words used to assure they are responding appropriately. But make sure it does not appear that you are glaring or staring at them. As seen earlier, micro-expression can be fleeting and missing them could result in incorrect conclusions about a response.

# Question Form

The two question forms are "Closed-Ended" and "Open-Ended" Questions. Each offers and requests a different kind of response style and each serves different purposes in an interview.

## Closed Ended (Direct) Questions

Closed ended questions are also known as direct questions because they provide a limited or closed pool of answers from which to choose. They are good for categorizing demographics and usually require very little thought. In most cases this means you should expect an immediate response. If a stalling action is used, this kind of question makes that effort more obvious. This question also magnifies stress, again making a deception easier to identify. Questions in which no delay should occur are questions such as "What city do you live in", "what is your last name", "how old are you", "are you married" and so on.

Closed ended questions are useful in clarification and verification. For example, "So, you are saying that X did Y, right?" This makes use of previous responses to questions of any type.

Directly asking a person a question they do not want to answer is likely to induce a deception (especially a lie). By asking the straight forward "Did you do it?" you have provided only two realistic answers: Yes and No. However, they may resort to other techniques in order to keep from outright lying so that they can mislead instead. For example, asking if a subject is Native American, you may get a response such as:

"Although, I am only ¼ Native American, I live in the old ways, so this is not a simple question". This kind of response buys the subject thinking time. Although the indicators of a stall and deception are present, the situation may result in an incorrect conclusion of deception. Why? Some people prefer accuracy on questions that are important to them. In the previous example the delay is not based on a deception, but a clarification in an effort to cooperate fully but carefully. This tendency to be careful in responses can be determine in the baseline setting or earlier responses if setting a baseline was not an option.

The rules of closed ended responses apply to typical American adults of normal intellect, presently free from intoxicating substances and not mentally disturbed.

On the other hand, juveniles, those under the influence of intoxicating or mood altering substances and the mentally impaired or disturbed are likely to respond in ways that vary from these general rules and as a result require specialized training for accurate evaluations.

Examples of Closed Ended Questions:
"Did you steal the Money?"
"You said you quit, so you're unemployed now?"
"Were you responsible for the accident?"

## Open-Ended Questions

An open-ended question does not force the subject to choose from a pre-selected set of possible answers. They ask questions that allow answers in full sentences and are often used to obtain new or additional information.

Generally, because open-ended questions allow open responses, they can be used to encourage a person to explain their views as they see them. This type of question can serve to decrease topic sensitivity and enhance rapport development as well as obtaining unknown information.

Also, when bringing up sensitive topics where deceit is likely, an open-ended question can encourage a truth-based deception (edited truth) over an outright lie – if deception is likely in the given situation. Generally, this provides a greater volume of information for analysis (embedded indicators of deception) than does a closed-ended question.

Although outright lies, such as those stemming from closed-ended responses, also contain indicators of deceit, they do not contain the amount of provided information for consideration. For example, if you ask, "Were you at home at 8:00 p.m.?" the response will more than likely be a simple 'yes' or 'no'. However, by asking, "Where were you at 8:00 p.m.?" you may get a complete statement of activities the subject was involved in. This could provide information that could be used to verify their claim or to obtain contradicting information leading to further inquiry.

As can be seen in the following open-ended questions, the potential responses may generate significant amounts of information: "What happened next?"; "How did you learn about that?"; "What else did you see?" etc.

Overall, when interviewing you must have an idea of the information you are seeking. If the goal is to obtain as much information as possible (such as when trying to determine whose story is honest) asking for information through open-ended questioning will produce more detailed and involved information and will usually contain a greater amount of indicators for use in making an determination of honesty or deception

# Question Function

## Introduction

While the type of question (closed and open-ended) direct the type of answer options, questions that serve a particular function are also quite useful. There are a variety of these 'function' questions, each with specific goals that serve the overall goal of information collection and verification.

Those most useful in Deception Management interviews include indirect questions (which divert the focus in sensitive areas of questioning); refocusing (which help keep an interview on topic); assumption (which help verify presumptions about unclear information); Clarifying (which encourages the subject to offer additional details while seeming to verify conclusions) and Statement Appraisal questions (which encourage the addition of any information that may not have been addressed, but seen as potentially important to the subject). Whether they have forgotten or were hesitant this approach gives them an easy way to complete anything they feel important.

## Indirect (Alternative Respondent) Questions

Indirect questions are used to improve responses when a highly sensitive topic may be so concerning and stressful that deceptive responses may be likely.

If a respondent seems to be stalling when asked a sensitive question, you can place the stress on the presumed opinions of others not present. This produces an indirect answer since the subject is providing an answer as though he or she is answering for how they believe others might respond.

The effectiveness of this approach is loosely based on the psychological approach of free association or imputing what is on their mind even when considering ambiguous content matter.

Asking the subject what some 'other' person or persons may say has a different level of sensitivity than asking what the subject personally would say. The advantage is that it allows the subject to provide answers to questions where a loss of face, low self-esteem, fear, or other adversity (real or imagined) might be avoided while still getting at the desired information.

For example, "What do you think your neighbors might say caused the fire?" Also if you were to ask, "Do you think racial hatred was behind this vandalism" but receive a politically correct response such as, "I wouldn't know, I am not prejudiced." Then you can ask, "What do you think the neighbors would say about whether this was racially motivated?" This approach is likely to get a different answer. Because they are not risking being labeled as a racist, they may offer an answer that contains their politically incorrect beliefs.

## Re-Directive (Refocusing) Questions

When a subject gets off topic in an interview, you must not ignore that effort. Knowing that "everything we do, we do for a reason", you can conclude the topic just prior to the avoidance tactic was so sensitive and caused such emotional discomfort, they felt the need to veer away from that topic. If you use a re-directive question, you can maneuver the subject back to the central focus of the interview and continue.

For example, if a subject that has been raped and strays from the topic by comments on how much she likes the shirt I'm wearing, asking the re-directive question, "Are my clothes similar to the clothes the rapist was wearing?" brings the discussion back to the focus of the interview.

If refocusing efforts are resisted, using a direct question to confront the avoidance attempt can manage the avoidance issue and get the interview back on target. For example, if the rape victim repeatedly seeks to avoid the topic, then using questions such as, "I know this is very stressful, but if you avoid talking about it we are allowing him to do this to other girls, do you want that on your conscience?"

## Assumption (Leading) Questions

To verify conclusions, make a statement that includes the given information along with your assumed conclusion and a question requesting them to verify the conclusion. For example, a subject states, "I wanted everyone to know that anything I thought about doing to myself was not their fault." This may possibly be their way of announcing they had been (and maybe still are) thinking about suicide. So, you might verify that conclusion by asking, "Am I right in thinking that you're considering suicide?

Frequently, interview comments lead you to a conclusion that was never clearly stated. Assumption questions are used to verify those conclusions.

This can be done through the use of leading statements that include your presumed conclusion as a stated fact. However, to avoid alerting the subject to the potential importance of such a conclusion (which might put them on the defensive), make the statement phrasing seem as though the assumption is already known AND not particularly important. Once the assumption is announced, the subject will verify or deny the assumed conclusions. Regardless, it may be quite important to underplay the significance of the topic.

Example: A comment is made about "having a good time while shooting some pool at "Red's Bar and Grill". Although they never stated they had been drinking, you assume that since they were at a bar,' having a good time' while shooting pool, they were probably having alcoholic drinks. The likelihood that they had a few beers (or drinks) while there is reasonable, but was not stated.

By asking, "When you left the bar, would you say that you had more or less than 8 beers?" This gets directly to the point. However, it also clearly puts the emphasis on the alcohol consumption. If the assumption is wrong then it is likely that the response would have been clearly identified as incorrect in that "I did not drink at all that night" or some similar strong denial.

Another approach would be, "So did your game (pool shooting skill) improve after a few beers, or get worse like mine usually does?" The response will give you the next move in the interview.

## Clarifying Questions

Clarifying questions seek to accomplish the goal of improving the amount of information obtained and verifying, refining or correcting the content achieved.

When information is vague, imprecise or ambiguous this question functions to clear up what it is lacking. For example asking; "I am unsure what you meant when you said you did not see her last night. Did that mean you did not see her at all or just during the nighttime?" may be used to seek specific information that was ambiguously provided. If the issue was something that occurred at a specific time, this could be vital information.

Additionally, when a subject seems to have run out of information to offer, asking them to verify your understanding of what has been stated up to this point can be very useful. In this case, stating something like, "Here is what I gather from your comments so far. If anything is not correct be sure to let me know." In both applications, this type of question accomplishes several objectives:

1. Encourage new, additional information (As I recite your comments, does any additional information or thoughts come to mind?).
2. Verification of information (Is this what happened?).
3. Elaboration of details (You were on a swing. How were you 'on a swing' – sitting, swinging, backward, standing etc.?).

An additional tactic that can be used to increase statement validity and content verification is to subtly 'slip' in incorrect information while recounting what was said. If they catch and correct the inserted errors the confidence in their statements will be improved.

## Statement Appraisal Questions

To obtain additional and complete information it is important when concluding an interview to ask if they can rethink the situation and see if there is anything that was overlooked, forgotten or they were unsure of mentioning because it seemed insignificant or unrelated. Remind them that, "it is better to say something twice, than forget to say it at all."

Although you will normally receive a simple 'yes' or 'no' response, they also come with processing narratives (statements made while thinking over what was said). Many people will repeat portions of their statement while processing, but those that are deceptive will usually remain careful in what they say at this point. By reading their kinesics and emotions during this time may reveal discrepancies previously unnoticed.

# 12 NOTE TAKING

## Introduction

As a basic part of the interview process, it is reasonable and desirable to keep and refer to notes as the interview progresses. How an interviewer goes about these activities can either enhance or damage the quality of the interview.

Unfortunately, most interviewers don't realize how influential such procedures can be on the interview and its conclusions. Using improper procedures may result in multiple problems such as invalid baselines, oppositional relations, damaged rapport, perceptions of unprofessionalism, misinterpreted and overlooked indicators of deception, fear, anger and more.

## Physical Arrangements

### Seating for Note Taking

As previously discussed in "Environmental Preparations", a variety of concerns were covered including how room arrangements such as location, lighting, decorations, distractions and furniture placement can influence the interview. However, because most interviewers arrange seating to accommodate note taking, they often ignore these rules and in doing so, violate important principles.

In a typical interview setting, chairs are placed on opposite sides of a centrally located table. This arrangement provides a writing surface, a location to place files, folders, drinks and other items. Unfortunately, this setting interferes with effective interviewing in several ways:

1. Furniture placement interferes with the ability to observe non-verbal behaviors.
2. If the interviewer focuses more on their notes than the interviewee,
3. The interviewee is able to construct deceptions without those indicators being observed.
4. The presence and location of the table creates a psychological barrier encouraging a perception of "you versus them".
5. Similarly, this antagonistic perception is enhanced when files, notes and other objects are also placed between the two parties. These objects may also cause unnecessary distractions.

Each of these limitations increase fear and stress which weaken rapport and ultimately interfere with the validity of information even if their behavior is compared to a previously established baseline.

When conducting an interview in a different location and environment – such as in a personal residence, the interviewer tends to arrange their seating based on a location that will make it easier to refer to and record notes. Alternately, they hold the notepad in one arm and write with the other, making it virtually impossible for the interviewee to see what is written.

## The Notepad

The notepad or folder used to manage reference materials and keep notes is a powerful symbol of control.

Consider the interviewee's perceptions in a typically conducted interview: The interviewer establishes rapport, sets a baseline, then indicates the "formal" interview is beginning by opening the notebook while verbally adding, "OK. Let's get started".

The process is reversed at the end of the formal interview, with the interviewer closing the notebook and announcing, "Well that's all I need for now."

The fact that these actions occur in concert subconsciously suggest the notebook and its contents are so significant they direct the interview process. The opening and closing actions serve as transitions identifying when circumstances shift from "friendly" to "formal" (opening) and from "formal" to "friendly" (closing).

## Managing the Notepad

When holding the notepad or when using a centrally placed table, the contents of the notepad are hidden from view sending a message that the recorded information may be negative or damaging.

If the interviewer is focusing their attention on the notepad, files or other objects, he or she is, again, not observing the subject's nonverbal communications. If they repeatedly refer to their notes and other materials, they appear unprepared and may be viewed as incompetent or unprofessional.

## Taking Notes

When an interviewer appears to be more attentive to his or her note-taking than paying attention to the interviewee, the interviewee may feel discounted or ignored; both of which damages rapport.

Similarly, if the note-centric interviewer suddenly becomes focused on the respondent, especially when highly sensitive topics come up, the sudden interest may cause the interviewee to see this sudden change of attention as concerning or even threatening (especially if they have a low self-esteem). This can lead to feelings of fear and/or anger, increased stress and more stress indicators being presented for non-deception reasons. This weakens any identified indicators, the baseline setting and damages rapport.

As an illustration, imagine being among a group of people in which one person is speaking to the others. This person has been looking at each other person in a normal, random fashion until she decides to mention that someone stole her ring.

At that very moment, she looks directly at you. When we suddenly become the focus of attention in a stressful environment, we often have a notable stress response for no reason other than suddenly being the target of their seemingly negative attention.

In short, while taking a few notes is good, the attention given to the task of taking notes can create unnecessary problems and send conflicting messages as well as producing incomplete and unreliable conclusions.

## Note Taking Guide (Note Taking Solutions)

### Preparing for Note Taking

### *Plan the interview*
1. Before the interview, determine what information is needed to satisfy the purpose of the interview.
2. Prepare the appropriate questions for those needs.
3. Order the questions according to the stress each may elicit.
4. Place an abbreviated outline of needed questions on the notepad with sufficient space under each to write a brief of their responses and your indicator codes.
5. Using an outline instead of full sentences improves your ability to stay on track if a distraction occurs.
6. Have prepared responses to questions that may be fear based – such as about the recording device, code words, etc. For instance, if they see the codes etc. and ask about them, simply respond that they are memory jogs, place markers, doodles, etc. This will suggest the marks are unimportant and their continued inclusions will be of little concern. If done casually, and by simply recording their responses and adding no obvious comments, you reduce their concerns.

### *Physical Arrangements*
**More Seating Information**

Whatever seating is available to you, make sure it is used to make the interviewee as visible as possible. If you have a table, use it as a side desk so that you are both sitting on the same side.

Alternately, sit just around the corner from the interviewee but again with the ability to clearly see one another. Use the corner of the table for your notepad, folders, drinks and other items making sure the notepad is visible and not hidden. Keep in mind that while you are able to observe their entire body, they can also see yours.

If you're using only chairs, arrange them so that they are 4-6 feet apart and allow high visibility. If it is necessary to have additional case information available, have it in a separate folder and refer to it only when necessary. When you need to refer to that information announce what you are looking for so as to reduce or defeat the concerns that may otherwise be generated.

If you use a recording device (video or audio) ask their permission or make it known along with an appropriate explanation such as, "I hope you don't mind but I have to record these interviews for training purposes". Then place the object where it is useful but out of the way.

One particular related research finding is that if an interaction may become evidence in court, the picture can alter the jury's opinion by how it is framed. In short, if the interviewer/interrogator is in the picture, the jury takes a confession as less valid, than if the only one in the picture is the person being interviewed.

## *Notepad Use*

Use the notepad as a tool not a control device. Try to open or access it as though it is unimportant. Disconnect it from important verbal markers. For example, ask, "Shall we begin?" and after they respond, then open or access the pad. Similarly, when finished, comment, "Well, I guess we are done. I appreciate your time." And then almost as an afterthought, close and put the pad away. Again making it seem like it is not the main point of the interview. This way it seems you are remaining in the "friendly" role throughout the process.

Glance at the notes for key words and when recording, write only key words and codes. Do not fixate on the notes, but glance back and forth from the notes to the interviewee as you tell them what you are writing. This visual check will appear as though you are verifying the information with them as you go.

## *Managing the Notepad*

Keep your notepad flat on your lap or flat on the arm of the chair to make it clear you are not hiding what you write. When holding the notepad place it on your lap, or if you must hold it up to write information, lay it back on your lap as you finish writing your notes between each section. This makes it appear as a tool, not as the central, most important item or action. Placing it flat on your lap between question responses makes the pad appear accessible and not secretive. By using this approach, you are able to spend more time making eye contact and observing the subject's body language which allows you to be more immediately responsive to bodily changes.

## *The Interview Sheet*

A properly prepared interview sheet allows the interviewer to determine the needed information, collect responses and concerning indicators - all with minimal distraction.

### *Codes for Concerning Indicators*

The two goals of an interview are identifying and verifying information. While recording interview related information, key indicators can be used to identify and track those indicators altering baseline behaviors. The codes should be few in number and simple to use. The following areas are those most likely to be encountered and the most useful for our purposes. Each concerning area is listed with a suggested code. Any and all can be modified according to application and preferences.

1. ANS Stress Indicators (S, SS, SS+) - Use "S" for each sign. If two occur together use "SS"; If more than 2 are presented in close proximity use "SS+"
2. Unexpected Mental Effort (T) – for use when the subject is appearing to think more deeply than expected or called for.
3. Avoidance (A) – Because there are many ways to avoid honest responses (stalls, control efforts, redirects, intimidations, hijacking, not answering the question asked, etc.) one symbol can be used as a memory jog while remaining simple.

4. Content Analysis Concerns (W) include many possible issues (bridging, baseline deviations, poor introductions, changing meanings, etc.). While the letter "W" to indicate concerning word usage may be insufficient by itself to elicit sufficient recall later, adding a letter can elaborate. For example W + B = word bridge, WD = Changing definition, WP = Missing pronouns, etc...
5. Mismatched Behavior (X) can refer to conflicting signals. Again adding a letter to increase clarity may be used.
6. When there is a need to return to an interview area or topic, use "R" for return for further information.

## *A Sample Interview Sheet*

Most recent position listed on application?

___Yes, All FT ___(A)___ positions were listed___

Reason for Leaving Position?

Disciplinary Actions (write ups etc.)?

Drugs/Alcohol Used on Job or Affecting Job (incl. prescribed)?

Other Comments About That Position?

## Note Taking Tips

As you interact, focus more on the interviewee than your notes. Make sure that as you take notes, you keep the subject as the primary focus of your attention. Use body mirroring to encourage familiarity (unless theirs is extreme). Lean a bit forward. Tilt your head slightly as you listen. Nod and give acknowledgements regularly to indicate interest in what they are saying.

Do not read when they are speaking. Keep fear and stress to a minimum through carefully selected words. Avoid stigmatized, value laden or emotion evoking words and phrases (such as "Recreational drugs" not "Illegal drugs" or "dislike" rather than "hate").

Be very aware of sensitive topics. When they do come up, be sure you do not alter your behavior so the issue seems more significant than others. This retains the veracity of the baseline.

Anytime you observe the subject expressing a strong emotion, if it is not associated with the interview question, it may be in response to something you unwittingly provided. If this occurs, try to determine the cause and explain that behavior, apologize, or whatever approach seems appropriate to return the interviewee to their baseline level of behavior.

Make notes as short as possible. Use their words, but record only the very basics of what was stated. Do not record each and every word. Add in meaningless doodles/letters keep the significant codes from standing out as obviously meaningful.

# 13 CONTROL

The goal of the interview is to obtain valid information. Once the interview is underway, it must keep moving forward, in focus, and under control. However, when a subject is providing a narrative response, as long as they remain on a relevant subject - let them continue. If they stray, but continue to produce quality information or continuing improves needed rapport, allow it to continue until it is no longer productive.

If they get off track, take advantage of what they have said by using it to redirect the focus back to the relevant topic. If the interviewee is persistent in redirecting the focus, they should be confronted to determine why they are doing so.

A consistent inability of the subject to stay on task may indicate one of two concerning issues: It may be an avoidance tactic or an effort to take control of the interaction. If the issue is a sensitive topic, there should be stress indicators that precede the diversion.

If the subject will not stay on track and the situation is one in which someone's life or safety may be at risk, directly addressing the avoidance may be the best way to get an immediate response. However, this will probably reduce rapport and very possibly result in a falsified answer (an outright lie).

A direct confrontation is best used when specific information must be collected and the interviewer is very practiced in identifying deception. In such a case, use direct questioning techniques such as asking yes or no questions.

If clarification is needed at any point, make a note and come back to it later or if it is not disruptive to the present flow of information, ask for clarification at the moment.

If you decide to return to a sensitive point, simply ask something like, "why is it you don't want to discuss ___?" or a more indirect approach might be something like, "What comes to mind when you think about that topic?"

If a question remains unanswered, make sure you allow sufficient time for them to contemplate their response and then reword the question and ask it again. You can soothe any concerns by simply using the Columbo approach and stating that you are a bit confused and need them to clarify the issue. By returning to the topic at a later time new and potentially pertinent information may be revealed. Also, factual contradictions may occur and reveal previously unidentified deceptions.

If straying off track seems to be a bid for control, identify and manage the control issue. The most common method for trying to usurp interview control is "role reversal" or reversing who asks and who answers questions. If you suddenly realize that they are now the one asking questions and you are the one answering them, you are facing role reversal.

Role reversal can be defeated by fielding a question in such a way that control is returned to you. For example, when asking about pay cuts resulting from declining profits, they respond with, "Don't you think that pay cuts are a bad way to treat employees?" You can reverse the question with, I am sure there is more to the situation than I know. How do you think the employees should deal with the declining profit situation?" This takes their question, gives a non-involved response and returns the control to you. Since you are using their question to form your own question, you are once again in charge of the interview.

While it is counter-productive to be confrontational in trying to regain control, you should not permit the subject to continually remain in control unless it is serving you in accomplishing your goals. If you cannot regain control, take a short break and resume the interview or find a reason to reschedule for a later time and bring the present interview to an end.

An exception to this is you are interviewing a victim. Allowing them greater control may decrease their discomfort as they recall the unpleasant events you need information on.

# Concluding the Interview

Where you end the interview varies from one situation to another. Regardless, the rule is to end the interview when you have the information you need. However, you should always try to identify a 'natural break' in interaction to bring the interview to an end. Prior to actually exiting the interview, you should always ask if there is any additional information they would like to add and when they have nothing else to offer, thank them and if appropriate, indicate that you may be speaking with them again.

## Concluding Remarks

Interviewing is a complex interaction between people to obtain information. The information gained is often the basis for important decisions.

Many people believe that interviewing is simply talking with someone in an 'interview setting' and that it is no more than aimless, polite conversation. Such an interview obtains little useful information and any decisions that result are based on nothing more than 'gut' feeling (or some other vague measure). However, a professionally trained interviewer can often obtain critical information that would otherwise not be available.

Conclusions that result from an interview are often the basis for hiring or firing as well as how to proceed when trying to resolve a criminal investigation. However, there are countless other possible uses as well.

# Analysis Procedure(s)

Make sure your conclusions are Evidence-Based Conclusions.

Anything else is gambling and guesswork.

## Analyze – Do not Interpret

Analysis is not interpretation. Analysis evaluates information according to standardized rules and guidelines. This way, you are being objective and your personal feelings and judgments are kept to a minimum.

If you apply standardized rules to the information, you can discover what is embedded in the statement regardless of your personal familiarity with the statement contents. In other words, by following the guidelines, any findings are the result of a process that is not limited to our personal experiences.

Interpretation is the concept of using your own personal experiences to give meaning to collected information. When you interpret, you base conclusions about the behavior of others on your personal point of view and experiences. Since each person's comments and statements are unique, possessing personalized definitions, hidden meanings and contexts people are unaware of, an interpretation is often incorrect.

## When More Information is Needed:

Since the interviewee has a unique and personal point of view, his or her description of events may reveal previously unknown perspectives. The gained knowledge from the analysis process provides three main advantages to the investigator: Identified Deceptions, Identified Topics of Concern and Other Interview Focusing Information.

# 14 ELICITING HONESTY

## Introduction

While the ability to obtain information is a direct result of understanding the rules of behavior, the following sections include guidelines that enhance the ability to be effective in eliciting honesty in deception prone situations.

Although interview settings are especially prone to deception, there are many other situations where deception is likely to happen as well. In general, the tips in this guide apply to situations where questions are asked and answers are provided.

Ways these techniques can be applied include both formal and informal interactions, human resource interactions (such as employment interviews) and investigative interactions (such as crime investigations, intake interviews, behavioral discovery interviews and interrogations). However, deception management can be used in most any interaction between people.

## Fear Management

Managing fear as part of deception management's honesty elicitation requires accepting several fear-based propositions:
1. As the main reason for deception, fear is already a part of the process.
2. Manipulation of fear is necessary.

3. Techniques of fear manipulation are based on an understanding of how fear influences behavior.

Directly addressing fear as a means of eliciting honesty will produce unreliable results. Fear is grounded in doubt and suspicion, merely addressing the issue is insufficient for alleviating those concerns. Since fear is a strong emotion, there will be considerable resistance to accepting the idea that their fear is misplaced or inappropriate. When trying to convince someone of something they do not already agree with, their level of acceptance is in direct proportion to the established level of interpersonal trust. Specifically, the stronger the rapport between the interviewer and the subject, the greater chance fear management efforts will succeed. In other words, the more I trust you, the greater the chance I will accept your propositions.

To achieve a maximum level of acceptance so that opinions are given sufficient weight in the decision to deceive process, trust through good rapport must be established. Without developing a good rapport, addressing the topic may result in focusing the subject's attention on fear rather than honesty. For example, if I say, "don't think about the color blue", the color blue will leap to mind.

To accomplish the fear management goal of removing or displacing fear (to reduce the cause for deception) the subject must be maneuvered through two stages of psychological adjustment: You must be persuasive in obtaining their cooperation (Rapport Development) and you must resist your personal views in order to eliminate bias. Keep in mind that for fear management to be effective it MUST occur very early in the interaction.

# Two Components for Eliciting Honesty

1. Recognizing deception prone situations
2. Discouraging deception as an option.

## Recognizing Deception-Prone Circumstances

What are the circumstances that lead to deception? Deception is primarily a response to fear.

Other causes of deception include the enjoyment of getting one over on others – a concept Paul Ekman refers to as "Duping Delight". However, this and any variations are infrequent causes of deception.

Most deception causing fear is when we are afraid of the potential consequences if others come to know the honest truth. When the subject believes an unacceptable response could inhibit their goals or be the cause of an adverse reaction they are potential deceivers.

A point of clarification is needed here: Fear is used to suggest many kinds of responses. While fear of incarceration might lead to deception, so does a fear of spoiling a surprise party. The situations are vastly different, but the result, as far as being a cause of deception, is essentially the same. This gives a great deal of insight into identifying deception prone situations.

How are deception prone situations identified? Since the primary motivator of deception is fear, any situation where fear can be expected, the potential for deception is significant.

Fear is the concern that something desired will not be achieved or obtained. Fear can represent a concern over not being hired, being mistreated, being turned down, revealing a secret, feeling shame, being prosecuted or persecuted and so on.

While determining the potential of deception in every situation is impossible, most can be evaluated for a fear potential because the concerns are usually obvious and involves clearly recognizable circumstances where loss or failure exist i.e. hiring situations and accusations of guilt.

Another way to evaluate deception potential is to identify the events that frequently result in a deception. For example, when we ask a direct question where an immediate response is expected, fear may result from lack of processing time to evaluate the risk of the question and the response. In other words, it is common for people to conclude that an undesirable response (punishment, persecution, undesirable opinion, rejection, etc.) may occur if we are honest but we feel we have insufficient time to review the potential risks. This is especially true if the question seems accusatory.

For example, as in many organizations led by a board, lower level employees are directed to avoid contact with the board members for fear the employee might communicate inappropriately (such as complaining).

An employee was asked to have lunch with a board member. Later her supervisor asks, "Did you talk with any board members?" Since the question seemed accusatory, was framed in a 'yes' or 'no' format (direct question) and the question did not invite any explanation opportunity, the employee responds with an immediate "No" fearing she would be disciplined if she said yes.

# Discouraging Deception as an Option

## Introduction - Basic Principles

Interactions that involve fear are preconditions for deception. In such deception prone situations, the subject fears the consequences they may face if they are honest. They may fear loss, pain, or failure to receive some desired gain. The fear that causes a situation to be 'deception prone' is potent and emotionally based. This is a powerful motivator that suggests honesty may not be the best choice.

## Eliciting/Encouraging Honesty

The primary way to accomplish honesty is to encourage honesty while discouraging deception. Honesty encouragement practices can be applied before entering a deception prone situation or after identifying and interrupting a deception that is being considered or is actually under construction.

Eliciting honesty is normally preferred over deception identification and confrontation because once a person has deceived, he or she will be very hesitant to recant the deception and rapport will be diminished. Also if a subject's deception is exposed, anger and defensiveness are likely to follow. However, even when using honesty eliciting techniques, the decision to deceive may still occur so the interviewer should always be on the lookout for signs of deception.

Because fear is the primary motive behind most deception, managing fear is vital to managing deception.

Fear is largely dependent on our perception of potential threat. If we believe a threat exists, our fear is based on three variables: the degree of the perceived threat, our vulnerability to that threat, and the credibility of that threat. Unfortunately, since fear is emotionally based, our evaluation of a threat is often an irrational action that is also emotionally based.

When people believe a realistic potential threat exists, they feel fear. The most effective approach for eliciting honesty is to transfer or remove fear.

## Fear Management

Fear management is the manipulation of fear in relation to the topic of concern. By altering or reframing perceptions concerning potential fears, we reframe the perception of fear by removing, minimizing, or shifting the fear to another issue, topic, or person. Because most people prefer to be honest if there is no reason to deceive, removing the fear from the issue will usually suffice.

Fear management is a two stage psychological process: Cooperation Enhancement and Fear Modification.

## Cooperation Enhancement

In order to convince a person to accept ideas, they must have reason to accept that what you have to say is worth considering. Establishing good rapport is the most effective way to coerce someone to consider your views as valid.

## Rapport

Rapport is the concept of having a harmonious connection with others. It is referred to as being 'in sync' or being on the same wavelength as the person you are interacting with. Rapport development and can greatly enhance relations and cooperation (including honesty). Rapport often occurs subconsciously which allows the ability to manipulate others through its positive aspects.

A survey of British detectives found that among failed interrogations (interviews seeking confessions); failure to establish a good rapport was the largest common element. When good rapport was established in follow-up interviews, they significantly increased the number of un-coerced confessions. Such is the power of rapport in the interview.

Rapport development usually begins with conversation, often through small talk. "Good Rapport" serves several useful and important functions in an interview:
1. It encourages compliance.
2. Its interactions make the subject more comfortable with you - the interviewer.
3. It enhances their psychological obligation to be honest.
4. It magnifies stress indicators if they are dishonest.
5. It assists in identification and evaluation of motivations, interests, and vulnerabilities.
6. It allows for a baseline setting in an unobtrusive and discreet manner.

## *Establishing Rapport*

There are a number of techniques beneficial to building rapport such as: matching your body language (i.e., posture, gesture, and so forth); maintaining eye contact; indicating interest with focused attention and matching breathing rhythm. Some of these techniques are explored in neuro-linguistic programming.

## *Persuading Rapport Acceptance*

**Persuasion** is the act of convincing someone to accept ideas, attitudes, or actions though the use of rationally and emotionally based encouragements. It is not the use of implied threats, force, pain, fear or coercion.

## Four Attributes of Persuasion:

There are four attributes of persuasion that can enhance the potential of cooperation: Likeable, Being an Authority, Reciprocating Confidential/Personal Information and Believing an Opportunity is Scarce and May Become Unavailable. Each strategy encourages cooperation in a different manner, but any and all can be used in concert to achieve the goal.

## Likeability

When people feel a rapport with the other person this generally indicates they like them. When you 'like' someone you automatically lower your guard, a very useful characteristic in encouraging and obtaining honesty. Although there is always someone you cannot please, most people can be swayed toward liking someone if that someone has the right characteristics or behaviors.

There are seven characteristic or behavioral factors found that affect likeability:

The first factor is the degree a person is considered to be physically attractive. Unfortunately, while some aspects of this are not within our control, there are many appearance related aspects that can be manipulated such as dress and cleanliness. To achieve maximum cooperation, putting forth the effort to be as attractive as possible (within the context of the situation) is very helpful.

The second factor is the perception that others appear to like you. When you obtain the sense that someone 'likes' you, you are much more encouraged to like them in return. These perceptions are often communicated both directly and indirectly. A major component of this factor is found within the rapport we establish with others.

The third factor in getting someone to like you is by simply behaving in a friendly and positive manner. People are almost always more responsive to a friendly and positive demeanor.

Fourth, people tend to like others that are similar to them. Giving the impression of this similarity encourages likability, cooperation and the decision to be honest. Similarity can be achieved by a large number of possible methods: Dress, use of terms, regional dialects, use of vocabulary, choice of pets, music preferences, past common experiences are among the many potential approaches to enhance the perception of similarity.

The fifth factor is when you believe the other person is familiar. Baseline setting and rapport development enhance this.

The impression that you are cooperative with the subject or at their interests is the sixth factor.

The seventh factor of likeability is achieved when you appear to possess positive traits (i.e. intelligence, competence, kindness, honesty, etc.). However, you must be careful to not appear generally superior. This can cause the opposite response.

## Being an Authority

The second identified strategy for persuasive influence is that of Authority. When people interact with someone, they tend to respect them (and are influenced by them) more if they see them as legitimately being an authority or an expert.

It must be noted, this is not the same thing as presenting oneself as a police officer when the subject is a suspect. Simply possessing power over another does not command respect.

People respect those they feel are trustworthy, that will be on their side and can add an air of expertise and authoritarian influence on their behalf.

## Reciprocity

The principle of exchange is a fundamental social law. People respond positively when they receive or expect to receive something and this can be promoted by offering something first. For instance, reveal something that seems to be significant. This suggests the possible presence of a trust or bond. Since we have been socialized to reciprocate, they will subconsciously feel they must obey social rules of behavior and respond in kind.

## Scarcity

While common in sales, the strategic tactic of restricting or limiting choices is a powerful motivator to action. In this case the action is cooperation or willingness to be persuaded. This is especially effective if an immediate decision must be made in light of losing the option. In other words, indicating that availability is lost if the offer is not immediately accepted.

Once a person has developed good rapport and established themselves as sufficiently reputable in the subject's eyes, he or she can move toward overcoming resistance they may face when trying to adjust the subject's fear and deception potential.

## *Additional Rapport Establishing Information*

### First Impressions "Presentation of Self"

Rapport begins with first impressions. Most people do not realize that first impressions are established in the first 1/10th of a second (primarily based on visual cues). These first impressions are then re-enforced and solidified or rejected within the first 10 seconds of actual interaction. It is very important to understand that once an impression is established, it is very difficult to change.

Do you convey confidence, wisdom, patience, or power, insensitivity, and a threatening atmosphere, or are you presenting an aura of weakness, insecurity, and disorganization? More importantly, which impression do you want to present? Once again, in the 1970's television show "Columbo", the title character always appears disorganized, unobservant, and weak minded. However, this was a purposeful misdirection to encourage others to feel overconfident.

In general, presenting an impression of professionalism is the best option. A 'professional' impression requires proper clothing and accessories, good grooming, style and demeanor. However, it should suggest minimum authority since an authority figure also produces an impression of judgment and even punishment. This 'authoritarian' impression reduces cooperation and will result in less information that is also of poorer quality.

Recent research has simplified the variables involved in establishing rapport. The research found that all the characteristics people use when evaluating a person when they first meet him or her can be summed up in two areas of consideration: Warmth and Competence. When you perceive a person to be both warm (friendly and well intentioned) and competent (the ability to actually accomplish one's intentions) the chances of establishing a positive rapport increases significantly.

### Face Saving

Losing face is the perception that a person loses their value in the eyes of others. Losing face is about disrespect, loss of prestige, self-confidence and even honor. Avoiding a 'loss of face' is also known as 'saving face'. Assisting someone in 'Saving Face' is potentially the most powerful and successful method of establishing or enhancing rapport.

To assist someone in saving face, you are allowing them to retain their respect and dignity in a situation that could be quite damaging. The act of face saving often results in a subject that is more cooperative and can open doors of communication that would otherwise remain closed.

Similarly, you can assist a person in saving face by assigning blame elsewhere when it seems they are to blame, by minimizing an issue that might reflect on them poorly, or even maximizing a negative about someone or something else so that the subject's actions pale in comparison. For example, if the subject is convinced they are ethically blameless (even if they are legally guilty) they will respond better and may believe they owe you one. You can also assist them by assigning blame for the situation on someone or some other circumstance.

In an employment situation another type of face saving can be used. For example: You want to interview an employee about a potential employee theft situation and they are the primary suspect, but when you locate them, they are in the company of others. You can gain respect from them (rapport) by announcing that you need their help in solving a problem. If you were to announce the real reason, they would be in a 'loss of face' situation that could result in their disgrace. Instead, assist them in saving face by announcing that you need their help and then announcing their role as a suspect in a more private setting.

If such an opportunity arises, take advantage of the ability for them to 'owe you one'. If necessary allow yourself to appear weak to others if it helps the subject avoid disgrace. Keep in mind that we often serve as our own audience, so face saving does not require the presence of others. By avoiding a situation where their self-perceptions may be damaged, you allow them to maintain their self-esteem.

The positive attributes of face saving are important. If the subject is in the company of others, providing face saving for the subject at the expense of looking weak to their associates will only strengthen the subject's opinion of you. In short, when assisting someone in saving their reputation, they will normally recognize the gesture, rapport will start off well and they may feel enough of an obligation to you that if they come to feel the need to be deceptive their stress indicators will be more obvious due to a sense of shame – as in "He did me right and now I am going to lie to him? That's pretty low."

## *Evaluating Rapport*

You can gauge your level of rapport in many ways. The most significant are body mirroring, interpersonal distances, verbal style and language content. When a person mirrors your stance, and body language, rapport is good. Another good rapport indicator is when the subject moves toward you (except in cases of obvious aggressive anger).

Alternately, when the subject distances themselves from you physically or verbally, they avoid eye contact or change their bodily position or stance in a manner that opposes yours, rapport is weak, weakening or absent.

Another sign of losing rapport would be if their language use toward you becomes shortened or less inclusive. For example, swapping inclusive phrases such as "why don't WE get some coffee?" with more distant phrases such as "why don't you have some coffee with me?"

## *Enhancing/Repairing Rapport*

When signs of rapport distancing are identified, damage control should be implemented. Although efforts to repair damaged rapport can be difficult if not impossible, rapport can oftentimes be improved by using appropriate body language (mirroring, leaning forward, maintaining a comfortably spatial distance) making sure these efforts remain consistent with your other actions (behaviors, words, and underlying demeanor) and so forth. Another approach is being attentive to the subject's needs and comfort (support, thirst, discomfort, etc.).

For example, using a casual relaxing interview following a high-tension traumatic situation may produce information otherwise not obtainable. Also, if rapport is altered negatively by your actions, offering sincere explanations of the circumstances and apologies can remedy the situation if the rapport weakening is the result of a misunderstanding.

As previously noted, persuasion is the process of guiding people in a positive manner toward the acceptance of ideas, attitudes, or actions based on rational and emotional appeals. The goal is to obtain honesty by persuading the subject(s) to make the decision to cooperate and do so with the belief they are making the choice through their own freewill.

Although persuasion can be a highly effective tool of manipulation, its use must always be tempered toward the single goal of seeking honesty. Inappropriate use of persuasion can result in many serious problems, such as false confessions.

# 15 RESPONDING TO DECEPTION

In the interview, one of the primary goals is to determine deception. After identifying a subject has been deceptive, you should do your best to conceal any emotional reactions (including surprise). Simply keep the information to yourself.

When lied to, you can decide to confront the subject or let them continue in their deception as a means to strengthen your position.

Once a deception has been identified and it is determined necessary to address it, keep in mind that accusing someone of lying is an automatic stress situation and will cause significant damage to rapport and possibly to the goals of the interview itself. Be especially aware that you should not reprimand the subject. Doing so will destroy all rapport, is a value judgment, insinuates you are not objective and creates an oppositional relationship.

Most people do not readily admit to having lied. However, if you decide it is useful or necessary to confront a deception, reveal it as a 'matter of fact' and provide face saving techniques that offer moral grounds for their deception (if maintaining rapport is needed).

Example: The subject lies about why he or she left a job. Knowing the previous employer is noted as being unfair, you could offer, "Lisa, I know John over at XY and Z and he informed me that you were fired for theft. However, because I know those people I also know that many times their hiring and firing practices are not quite what they claim. We have had excellent employees that came from there with similar situations. I know every story has two sides and I want to know yours. Can you explain to me exactly what happened?"

# Identified Topics of Concern

When indicators from the investigation point to specific topics as being concerning and they are relevant to the goal of the investigation, you should follow up on those topics to determine if they contain important or useful information. Since they were identified through indicators, there is a strong likelihood they in fact do have a strong significance.

For example, in an interview the subject stalls in responding to the question, "Have you ever tried any recreational drugs other than alcohol?" You are aware they have not made any other stalling efforts in other areas and response hesitancy was not indicated during baseline setting. All this suggests that drug use other alcohol is the cause for concern. Do not assume it is because they are a drug user. For all you know (until you ask further) they may have had a relative or close friend who was seriously impacted by drug use and any discussion about that topic brings to mind events they do not like to think about.

However, since alcohol and other drugs were mentioned, you must isolate the parts of the topic to identify which specific is the cause of the indicator (See also micro-bridging). Asking questions about each one can lead to the specific concern. The ones not the source should have replies in accordance to their baseline behaviors.

Beginning with the least concerning, alcohol – since it is a legal drug, it is less likely to be the cause of the problem. Once alcohol has been eliminated, move to the next stress level drug such as prescribed medications. By separating each part of the question, indicators can be gauged and any real concerning areas can be noted.

# Investigate External Information

When the investigation/interview reveals information that can be externally verified the investigator must follow-up on that information to confirm its accuracy. If it is confirmed as inaccurate, it suggests the subject felt a need to provide false information. The goal then is to determine why the deception was provided and whether it relates to the goal at hand.

# Verifying Information

There are two forms of verification: Clarification and Substantiation. Clarification is a request for their help in determining if what you have learned is what they thought they were communicating. It is important that as you request clarification you allow the subject to speak without interruption or distraction. Never put words in their mouth or thoughts in their brain. Let them provide all the information.

The second approach is to verify noted facts. When the interview provides information externally verifiable (such as claims of being at a specific store at a specific time – something that may be verified by store security or by employees that were working at the time), it is important to do so since such information is objective and may provide additional information.

If they mention they were at a movie, you can check it out later or verify it immediately. To verify it immediately, interject a variable they must respond to. For example, if they mention a movie, ask them what movie and where. After they respond, interject with questions about how they dealt with some issue such as, "I know the street flooded due to a broken water main and they were having patrons enter and exit through the side doors. Which side did you use?" Since there was no broken water main, if they were actually at the movie, they will announce something to the effect of, "they let us in the front, I didn't see any evidence of a flood" or they may answer deceptively, such as, "They had everyone enter through the West door and leave through the East exit."

# 16 OVERCOMING RESISTANCE
## (Fear Modification & Honesty)

## Introduction

In Deception Management '**resistance**' is defined as the inclination to avoid being honest. A person's resistance can be determined by two factors: Their level of fear about potential consequences and the importance of the situation.

It is very important the anti-resistance approach is carefully chosen. Selecting the wrong approach can destroy rapport and ruin any effort to defeat or inhibit deception. For instance, if coercion is used, the subject's resistance will significantly increase and the likelihood of deception may also significantly increase. If the goal is to increase emotional responses (such as with specific applications of emotion recognition) then coercion should be very effective.

However, there are several approaches that can be useful and effective in reducing the potential of deceit in deception prone situations. These include using Fear Displacement, Fear Reduction, Depersonalizing, Commitment and Consistency, Distracting and Disrupting (Mental Interference), Social Validation and Acknowledge and finally Confrontation (fear). The following description of each approach and its application is listed in order of usefulness.

# Fear Displacement Introductions

Displace fears by refocusing concerns. When desiring to promote truthfulness as you interact, you must inhibit deception by recognizing what parts of the interaction will be deception prone and applying fear management techniques accordingly. Since each interaction is unique, there is no "always correct" approach. For example, talking in a social setting is considerably different than conducting a job interview or an investigation.

To incorporate fear reduction techniques, timing is important. Essentially, the technique must be applied before raising areas of concern. In an interview, the concerning areas are often discussed one at a time and the fear management tactic can be applied as each area is being introduced. However, as you apply the technique, it is important to not contaminate the information with personal bias. Contamination often occurs without conscious intention. Comments indicating bias, body language, vocal inflections and so on can be picked up by the interviewee who may adapt their responses to that bias.

The goal is to prepare the subject so they experience no 'shock' as you begin asking questions associated with an area. This approach improves the ability to attach identifiable stress to a specific question rather than having the possibility that the identified stress is a surprise reaction to the topical area. This tactic makes the subject more sensitive to the importance of each section, makes them familiar with the contents, and as a result, magnifies emotional reactions so that when a deception does occur, it is more easily identified.

Fear Displacement Introductions are statements made prior to questioning about a topical area which may be potentially deception prone. The goal is to replace their fears related to the specific topics with concerns about being identified as dishonest.

This is done in a two stage process:

1. Make the Concerning Topic a Non-Issue – Make it clear that no one is (or is expected to be) completely innocent of wrongdoing and those events are not the focus of the questioning.

2. Make Honesty the Issue - Prior to asking the topic related questions, make it clear that the primary goal, above all else, is honesty and ANY dishonesty will result in the worst case scenario in the given situation – such as not being hired, being fired, etc.

Example: When interviewing applicants for a position as a courtesy driver, announce that it is a fact that most everyone goes over the speed limit from time to time and having done so is an expected and normal behavior. However, personal integrity is the most concerning issue since the well-being of the clients is the utmost and being honest is seen as an indicator of integrity.

## Procedure

In your planning and preparations, divide the interview into areas or topics of concern. Use the two stage process (above) as you enter each topical area. Question sets of topical areas should be introduced in such a way as to encourage truthfulness (see Fear Displacing). Prior to starting, you should emphasize the fact that there are positive effects of honesty, negative effects of dishonesty (all forms of deception) and that procedures are in place to verify gained information so they gain a sense that if they deceive, they will be caught.

At the same time indicate through fear reduction that the concerning area is actually of little significance. In brief, the chance of getting caught in a deception is good and will result in an undesirable outcome. However, emphasize the idea that the most important issue is truthful answers and their importance seriously over-rides any concerns.

Reinforce the understanding that no one is expected to be perfect. Reinforce the importance of honesty being the primary concern regardless of minor past judgments.

## Fear Reduction (Reducing Concern)

Fear (resistance) control can be accomplished by reducing or removing apprehension that led to their fear.

This is accomplished by providing them with information that makes their fears unjustified. The primary methods to achieve this are:
1. Indicating the behavior or issue causing their fear is actually a normal and expected circumstance and the reason for their concern is unfounded.
2. Indicating their circumstance is concerning only if it exceeds some exaggerated amount or severity. Since the level used for comparison is significantly exaggerated, their concern is greatly reduced also reducing the felt need to deceive about it.
3. Depersonalize the situation so that the subject believes they are not being 'personally' judged.

The circumstances and the particular behaviors dictate which approach should be applied in any given interaction. Keep in mind overuse of any such tactic will result in a loss of trust and effectiveness.

## Overcoming Fears

While reducing and eliminating fear is the preferred choice for obtaining honesty, there may be circumstances where these are not the best options or for some reason will not work. If this is the case, use other methods to manipulate the person into being honest. The primary methods to achieve this are:

1. Many people fear negative evaluations of themselves on a personal level. By making it clear that the situation is not personal, the fear is reduced.

2. When someone makes a statement of dedication to a set of principles, ethics or morals, their allegiance can be used as leverage to encourage honesty.

3. As we determine whether to deceive or not, we mentally evaluate the situation for options. If the situation does not require a very immediate response, the person will seek to fully evaluate the situation and decide whether to lie. Interrupting this decision process can encourage honesty.

# Normalization of Behavior

Normalize Concerning Behaviors by making it seem as if concerning behaviors are normal and expected.

Normalizing Behavior is the practice of removing the fear of admitting to a behavior by making that behavior either seem normal and even expected or seem minor in comparison to what is announced as concerning behaviors, or levels of behaviors.

During most interviews a sensitive subject will usually have to be discussed. In most cases it is a topic that threatens the subject's agenda in the interview. For instance, in an investigation, the subject will be concerned about issues that might suggest guilt. In an employment interview the concern will be about issues that would affect getting hired. In either case the subject may become so concerned that they believe the best option is to try to deceive. This fear based deception will usually be identifiable through indicators, most especially a stalled response when a known potentially sensitive topic is brought up.

To effectively manage this potential deception, the interviewer must reduce the concern of the interviewee. By intervening and using comparative normalization, the interviewer can elicit more information from the subject by creating an artificial safety net for unacceptable behaviors.

Comparative normalization is very effective if properly and wisely used. This approach is a method of effectively desensitizing a topic of concern by making it clear that such a behavior is considered relatively normal, as is typically found among people and such behavior is understandable while deception is unacceptable.

For example, it is well known that in today's society, people drink, experiment with or use drugs in a social context on occasion, shoplift at some point in their life and so on. The idea is to suggest these behavioral flaws as not all that important but dishonesty is and it will result in negative outcomes. This places the concern on deceiving and motivates the subject to reveal answers which more closely approach the truth.

This approach used appropriately and not overused, is generally effective. However, it should be practiced only where there are clear indications that deception is being considered such as when there is an effort to stall before answering a sensitive question.

Once a stall is identified, interrupt the deception decision process (minimizing or cognitive loading). This defeats the stall.

Whatever question was last asked is the question that should be addressed. Implementing persuasion tactics of 'reciprocating personal information' can be useful – such as stating that, when I was younger I tried the 'wacky weed a few times. Heck everyone I knew then did too."

If drug use was the topic, a reminder to the subject that minor drug use is something that most people have at least tried and is little concern. Similarly, such questioning the question should not be phrased as 'yes' or 'no' questions but as, questions of 'which', 'when', 'how much', 'how many' etc. For example, instead of asking have you ever tried marijuana, you should ask, how many times have you tried marijuana in the last (year, 5 years, month) whatever time frame you select.

## Exaggerated Comparisons

As with normalizing, the Exaggerated Comparisons technique is designed to reduce the sensitive nature of the topic (reducing the need to feel fear) by claiming that only exaggerated levels of involvement (in whatever topic being covered) is concerning. This by comparison makes most other levels of involvement seem insignificant. This is carried out by making a statement where almost absurd levels of involvement are the real concerns.

For example, in an employment interview one of the concerns has been people inappropriately taking sick days off. You begin desensitizing by verbally announcing that, "everyone gets sick, that is why we have sick days. We know that some employees take an occasional sick day off as a mental health day when they built up a large number of days and haven't been using them." Then continue with the exaggerated comparisons; "Unfortunately, we have had some employees that take advantage of our tolerance by taking two and even three weeks off at a time claiming they were sick when the reason was taking a vacation."

After indicating what a serious level is, ask how many times they have been involved in the issue at a slightly less exaggerated level, and how many times have you taken more than a week off at a time for non-medical reasons." Using the phrase "more than" insinuates the level mentioned is an imaginary dividing line of concern. Since most applicants will never have inappropriately taken this much time off, they will likely respond with "Never!"

However, if they provide a response other than never, you may decide you need to know more on this point and then you must identify how much they actually did take off and why. "Well, how many days have you taken off for non-medical reasons?"

You may get a response of none, or some other level of response. They will not need thinking time if their response is none. So if they take thinking time before that answer they are probably lying. If they give another answer, there is a high likelihood the actual number is higher than the amount they provide.

If it seems they have to think too deeply to come up with an answer, interrupt with a number for them to compare to, "Well, have you taken more than three or four days' at a time?" At this point, the stall indicates a deception was potentially being considered and the response likely to be lower than reality. Accept the range produced and move on since precision is unnecessary as the real goal was to determine any involvement at all.

In the end, you should congratulate and reassure them that their honesty greatly supports their future chances, even if this is not true. Positive reinforcement is the best method for assuring a desired behavior will be repeated (in this case, honesty).

To make full use of this approach, make sure you do not follow up with any comments that will indicate you were not honest in your comments about concerning levels or all rapport will be lost.

## Depersonalize the Situation

Another approach to reduce the fear about a topic is to depersonalize the situation. Discuss how others managed the situation (use both honesty and deceptive examples) and describe how it turned out for them. Then suggest if they want a positive outcome, they emulate the person who accomplished the positive outcome (was honest even when it seemed concerning).

## Use Identified Commitments

Another strategy to influence or achieve cooperation is to couch your goal request in a format or manner that is consistent with (or at least not in opposition with) a position they previously identified with. This includes any statements or declarations of ethics, motivations, or principles.

If the interviewer can encourage a commitment to doing something, it can be used as leverage to achieve some follow through. This is, at least partially, behind the counseling approach of behavioral contracts.

If these previously made commitments are available, they can be used to encourage cooperation by appealing to their own beliefs or values. For example, a gang member might be motivated by using their allegiance to his or her gang and its principles by requesting their cooperation. They would do this as a means to provide the gang with a sense of being right and justified in some action or belief.


## Interfere with the Deception Process

Interrupting a deception requires recognizing the situation as deception prone or recognizing the processes a subject uses when they are in manufacturing their deception.

**Mental interference** is the tactic of reducing deception by interfering with the deception decision or creation processes. People prefer to deceive by manipulating factual information, because it gives them time to mentally process the facts in preparing their deception.

Distraction interrupts the thinking process (also discussed under "Internal Dialogue"). Adding mental tasks at this time (also known as 'cognitive loading') interferes by causing a mental speed bump. This can be as simple as interrupting with a question that requires a specific detail.

For example, the concern is where was an employee at 8:00 (when the power went out and money was stolen from a cash register). The subject is asked where they were, and as soon as there are indications of possible deception creation (unnecessary stalling, internal dialogue, pupil dilation, etc.) the interviewer asks, "Who else was clocking in when you did?" or "Exactly when did you clock in?" these occupy their mind taking the mental effort from the deception decision/creation process. If the main question is restated as the person is thinking about the interjected question, they will have to respond or their deception effort will be magnified.

Just as when you are looking for a street address while driving and someone with you is asking – "Are we there yet?"; "Is that the place?" and "When are we going to get there?" Each question interferes with the concentration process causing frustration and even anger. Similarly, this is why we tend to turn down the radio in these situations.

## Use Social Validation (Conforming to Group)

Humans are social animals, and believing others humans have been persuaded to accept some belief or perform some action, is strong encouragement to follow suit themselves. The urge to do so is enhanced when those 'others' are similar in various ways (e.g., age, race, interests, socioeconomic status, etc.) and if they were many in number. For example, when a crime by multiple offenders is under investigation, one suspect is more likely to provide information if he believes others of his group have already done so.

## Acknowledge and Confront the Potential for Deceit

If you acknowledge and confront the potential of deception in upcoming interviews or about specific topics, you can intercept the concern that motivates the potential deception and/or replace them with concerns about deceiving. By doing so, the motivation to deceive is replaced with motivation to prove their integrity.

Keep in mind that research suggests these techniques may only work for people prone to deceive or resist suggestions. Thus, this approach can be especially useful with adolescent subjects.

For example, stating something like, "I know it may be tempting to simply say what you think I want to hear, instead of just being honest, but . . . ." or "You know most interviewees think that if they appear perfect, they will increase their chances of being hired but . . . ."

If the interview is something other than an employment application and deception seems likely, a more direct approach using "reverse psychology" (also known as "paradoxical intention") can be effective. In this tactic, the goal is to manipulate a likely deceiver into wanting to reject any negative views held about their honesty and integrity.

By acknowledging that you expect deception, a resistant subject is motivated to prove you wrong by being honest. For example using an introduction such as, "I know that you have reasons to think you should not cooperate or be honest, but …"

# 17 Deception Management

Deception Management evaluates, extracts, refines and combines the most valid approaches to deception identification. This allows for success rates much higher than previous possible.

In the development of the Deception Management approach, several steps had to be completed. First, the most effective and usable methods of deception identification presently known had to be identified. This step included areas other than strictly deception related since much of a person's total communication system is hidden messages and their meanings.

The next phase was the extraction and streamlining of the most effective contents within those selected approaches (based on independent research).

Once identified and streamlined, the research technique known as triangulation was applied. This approach merges the various methods into a system where the weaknesses of each method are made up for by the strengths of the other methods. This allows a trained investigator to select the techniques best suited to a situation, and by using the comparative analysis approach of deception management, potentially achieving success rates above 90%.

## Final Considerations

The ability to positively identify deception has been sought for centuries. We have tried to find or create a reliable and valid way to detect lies. Unfortunately, we have not succeeded.

There have been a multitude of promising approaches such as body language analysis, statement analysis, behavior modification and theme development interviewing, handwriting analysis, stress identification machines (polygraphs and voice stress analyzers), and many others. Still, while some are a bit better than guessing, every method has severe weaknesses causing them to be unreliable. This lack of reliability can result in an honest response being incorrectly labeled a lie.

When a test produces flawed results, some investigators believing the test is foolproof will resort to applying various forms of pressure to support the conclusion that there was no flaw (such as when seeking a criminal confession). These incorrect beliefs combined with fears and (if in the legal system) the option of plea bargaining, all too often produce false confessions. An additional and unfortunate impact is that when a test is failed, the labeled 'liar' suffers social persecution and often is unfairly discriminated against in employment and other socially based interactions.

## Concluding Thoughts

The refinement and merging of the dominant methods as provided in Deception Management Training allows an investigator to avoid the problems common to most training programs. These problems include long training sessions that incorporate unnecessary filler, anecdotal experiences offered as valid techniques, overly detailed and specific applications unusable by most participants, and in some cases the presentation of fabricated data used to support personal views.

These problems waste time, reduce success through information overload and false discriminatory indicators, confuse content and are sometimes contradictory. This is further exacerbated with the fact that most of those trained in a deception identification technique rely on a single method as their basis for conclusions.

Not only can these pitfalls be overcome by applying the Deception Management approach of multi-modal training, deeper levels of knowledge are gained and success rates are dramatically increased.

# Referenced Materials

Adams Susan H. (Oct. 1996). The Art and Science of Criminal Investigation: Statement Analysis: What Do Suspects' Words Really Reveal? FBI Law Enforcement Bulletin, Oct. 1996.

Adams Susan H. (April 2, 2002). Communication Under Stress: Indicators Of Veracity And Deception In Written Narratives. Doctoral Dissertation - Virginia Polytechnic Institute and State University.

APA-a -- American Psychiatric Association. 1994. Diagnostic and Statistical Manual of Mental Disorders (Fourth Edition). Published by American Psychiatric Association. Washington, DC. Note: referred to in text as APA-A.

APA-b (American Polygraph Association) CVSA Position Statement. polygraph.org/ voice.htm. June 2000.

Augustine, Saint (1952). Treatise on Various Subjects. (Deferrari, Roy Joseph, ed.) Washington D.C. Catholic University Press.

Bailey Frederick George 1988. Hambuggery and manipulation: The art of leadership. Ithaca NY Cornell University Press.

Bandura, Albert (1979). The Social Learning Perspective: Mechanism of Aggression. Psychology of Crime and Criminal Justice ed. Hans Toch New York. Holt, Rinehart, & Winston.

Barnes, J. A. (1994). A Pack of Lies: Toward a Sociology of Lying. Cambridge University Press.

Ben-Shakhar, Gershon and John J. Furedy (1990). Theories And Applications In The Detection Of Deception: A Psychophysiological and International Perspective. Springer-Verlag Publishers New York 1990

Bennis, W. G.; Berlew, D. F., Schein. E. H. and Steel. F. 1. (Eds.): Interpersonal Dynamics, Essays and Readings on Human Interaction, 3rd ed. Homewood, Dorsey Press, 1973.

Binder. D. A., and S. C. Price (1977). Legal Interviewing and Counseling. St. Paul, West.

Bjork, Elizabeth L. & R. A. Bjork (1996). Memory. San Diego. Academic Press, Inc.

Black, Max (1983). The prevalence of humbug and other essays. Ithaca NY Cornell University press.

Bok, Sissela 1978 Lying; Moral Choice in public and private life. New York. Pantheon Books.

Bowers, David A.: Systems of Organization. Ann .Arbor, University of Michigan Press, 1976.

Bull R: Can training enhance the detection of deception? in Credibility Assessment. Edited by Yullie JC. Dordrecht (Netherlands), Kluwer Academic Publications, 1989, pp 83-99.

Bynum, Jack. E. and William Thompson (1999). Juvenile Delinquency: A Sociological Approach. Allyn and Bacon. Boston, USA.

Conniff, Richard (Jan. 2000). " Letters" Discover Magazine. Volume 21 No. 1. Buena Vista Publishing Group. U.S.

Cooley, Charles Horton (1922). Human Nature and the Social Order. New York. Charles Scribner's Sons.

Cuddy, A. J. C., Fiske, S. T., & Glick, P. (2008). Warmth and competence as universal dimensions of social perception: The Stereotype Content Model and the BIAS Map. In M. P. Zanna (Ed.), Advances in Experimental Social Psychology (vol. 40, pp. 61-149). New York, NY: Academic Press.

Davidson, P.O. (1968) Validity of the Guilty Knowledge Technique: The Effects of Motivation. Journal of Applied Psychology 1968 Vol 52 No 1 62-65. American Psychological Association. Inc.

Davis, Flora: Inside Intuition. New York, New American Library, Times Mirror; 1975.

Demos, Raphael 1960. Lying to oneself. Journal of Philosophy 57:588-595.

DePaulo, Bella and Robert Rosenthal 1979. Telling Lies. Journal of Personality and Social Psychology. 37:1713-1717.

DePaulo BM, Lanier K, Davis T (1983): Detecting the deceit of the motivated liar. J Pers Soc Psychol 5:1096-1103, 1983

DePaulo BM, Stone JI, Lassiter GD: (1985) Telling ingratiating lies: effects of target sex and target attractiveness on verbal and nonverbal deceptive success. J Pers Soc Psychol 48:1191-1203,

DePaulo BM, Tang J, Stone JI: (1987) Physical attractiveness and skills at detecting deception. Personality and Social Psychology Bulliten 13:177-187, 1987

DePaulo PJ: (1988). Research on deception in marketing communications: its relevance to the study of nonverbal behavior. Journal of Nonverbal Behavior 12:253-273, 1988

DePaulo BM, Kirkendol SE: (1989) The motivational impairment effect in the communication of deception, in Credibility Assessment. Edited by Yuille JC. Dorchdrecht (Netherlands), Kluwer Academic Publications, 1989 pp 51-70

DePaulo BM, (1992): Nonverbal behavior and self-presentation. Psychological Bulletin, 111, 203-243.

DePaulo BM, Epstein JA, Wyer MM: (1993) Sex differences in lying: how women and men deal with the dilemma of deceit, in Lying and Deception in Everyday Life. Edited by Lewis M, Saarni C. New York, Guilford, 1993, pp 126-147

DePaulo, Bella M., J J. Lindsay, B. Malone, L. Muhlenbruck, K. Charlton, and H Cooper (2003). "Cues to Deception". Psychological Bulletin American Psychological Association. 2003, Vol. 129, No. 1, 74–118

Devitt, Mary K. C. R. Honts, and L. Vondergeest, (1997). Truth or Just Bias: The Treatment of the Psychophysiological Detection of Deception in Introductory Psychology Textbooks. The Journal of Credibility Assessment and Witness Psychology. 1997 Vol. 1 No. 1 9-32.

Dexter, Lewis Anthony: Elite and Specialized Interviewing. Evanston. Northwestern University Press, 1970.

Dick, D., Found, B. & Rogers, D. (2000). The forensic detection of deceptive behavior using handwriting movements. Journal of Forensic Document Examination, 13, 15-24.

Dillingham, Christopher. (1995).Traditional v. modern interview techniques. The Chief of Police, 2, 60-62.
Dillingham, Christopher Robert II. (1998) Would Pinocchio's Eyes Have Revealed His Lies?: A Study Of Eye Movements As Indicators Of Deception. Masters Thesis. University of Central Florida. Orlando, Florida
Downs, Cal W., Smeyak, G. Paul, and Martin, Ernest: Professional Interviewing. New York, Harper & Row, 1980.
Drake, John D.: Interviewing for Managers - Sizing up People. New York, American Management Association, 1972.
Eck, Marcel (1970). Lies and Truth. New York. Macmillan Pub. New York.
Ekman, Paul 1985. Telling lies: Clues to deceit in the market place, politics, and marriage. New York. Norton Pub.
Ekman P. (1981): Mistakes when deceiving. Ann N Y Acad Sci 364:269-278.
Ekman, Paul; Maureen O'Sullivan, Wallace V. Friesen, and Klaus R. Scherer (1991). Face, Voice, and Body In Detecting Deceit. Journal of Nonverbal Behavior Vol. 15, No. 2 (Summer 1991).
Ekman P, O'Sullivan M (1991): Who can catch a liar? Am Psychol 46:913-920.
Ekman P, (1989). Why Kids Lie. New York Charles Scribner's Sons
Ekman, Paul and W. Friesen. Facial Action Coding System: A Technique for the Measurement of Facial Movement. Consulting Psychologists Press, Palo Alto, 1978.
Ekman, Paul. Emotions Revealed: Understanding Faces and Feelings. Orion Publishing Group, Ltd. Psychologists Press, Palo Alto, 1978.
Ekman P, and W. V. Friesen (1972). Hand Movements. Journal of Communication 22, 353-374.
Elliot GC: Some effects of deception and level of self-monitoring on planning and reacting to a self-presentation. J Pers Soc Psychol 37:1282-1292, 1979
Farwell, Lawrence A. (2001). Farwell Brain Fingerprinting: A new Paradigm in Criminal Investigations. www.brainwavescience.com.
Ford, Charles V. (1996). Lies, Lies, Lies: The Psychology of Deceit. American Psychiatric Press. Washington, DC.
French, Scott and Paul; Van Houten (1987). Never Say Lie. CEP Inc. Boulder, CO. Criminal interrogation and confessions
Ganaway, G. K. (1989). Historical truth versus narrative truth: clarifying the role of exonerous trauma in the etiology of multiple personality disorder and its variants. Dissociation 2:205-220, 1989
Gil Luria, Sara Rosenblum. Comparing the handwriting behaviours of true and false writing with computerized handwriting measures. Applied Cognitive Psychology, 2009; n/a DOI: 10.1002/acp.1621
Goffman, Erving 1956. The Presentation of self in Everyday life (monograph2). Edinburgh, University of Edinburgh, Social Sciences Research Center.
Goffman, Erving 1975. Frame Analysis: an essay on the organization of experience. Harmondsworth: Penguin [17].
Goleman, Daniel (1982). Can you tell When Someone is Lying to you? Psychology Today 1982
Goldman-Eisler, F. (1968) Psycholinguistics: Experiments in spontaneous speech. New York. Doubleday.

Gorden, Raymond L.: Interviewing Strategy, Techniques, and Tactics. Homewood, Dorsey Press, 1969, 84, 188.

Hall, E. T.: The Hidden Dimension. New York, Doubleday, 1966.

Hall, Granville S. (1890). Children's Lies. American Journal of Psychology. 32:59-70.

Harding, Stephen and David Phillips 1986 Contrasting Values in Western Europe: unity, diversity, and change (Studies in the contemporary values of modern society) London. Macmillan.

Harrison AA, Hwalek M, Raney DF, (1978). Cues to deception in an interview situation. Social Psychology 41:156-161.

Hayano DM: Communicative competency among poker players. Journal of Communication 30:113-120, 1980

Hayano DM: Dealing with chance: self deception and fantasy among gamblers, in Self-Deception: An Adaptive Mechanism? Edited by Lockard JS, Paulus DL. Englewood Cliffs, NJ, Prentice-Hall, 1988, pp 186-199

Hess, John, (1997). Interviewing and Interrogation for Law Enforcement. Anderson Publishing Cincinnati OH.

Höfer, E., G. Köhnken, R. Hanewinkel, and C. Bruhn, (1992). Diagnostik und Attribution von glaubwurdigkeit. Kiel: Final report to the Deutsche Forschungsgemeinschaft, KO 882/4-2.

Honts CR, Raskin DC, Kircher JC: Mental and physical counter-measures reduce the accuracy of polygraph tests. J Appl Psychol 79:252-259, 1994

Inbau, Fred; Reid, John; and Buckley, Joseph (1986): Criminal Interrogation and Confessions. 3rd Ed. Baltimore, William. & Wilkins, 1986.

Johannesen, R. L. (1990). Ethics in human communication. Prospect Heights, IL: Waveland Press.

Kaminsky, A. R. (1974). Handwriting Analysis. Phoenix: O'Sullivan Woodside & Co.

Keifer, Richard W. (Feb. 7, 1998). American Polygraph Association official position on Voice Stress Analysis. http://www.polygraph.org/apa5.htm#what. World Wide Web.

Kleinmuntz, Benjamin: Essentials of Abnormal Psychology. New York, Harper & Row, 1974.

Klienmuntz, Benjamin and J. J. Szucko (1984a). A field study of the fallibility of polygraphic lie detection. Nature 308:449-450, 1984a

Klienmuntz Benjamin and J. J. Szucko (1984b). Lie detection in ancient and modern times: a call for contemporary scientific study. Am Psychol 39:766-776.

Klienmuntz Benjamin and J. J. Szucko (1981) B: Statistical versus clinical lie detection. Am Psychol 6:448-496.

Knapp, M. L., R. P. Hart, and H. S. Dennis (1974). An exploration of deception as a communication construct. Human Communication Research 1, 15-29.

Knapp, Mark: Non-Verbal Communication. New York, Holt, Rinehart, and Winston. 1972.

Köhnken, G. (1987). Training police officers to detect deceptive eye witness statements: does it work? Social Behavior 2:1-17, 1987

Köhnken, G. (1989); Behavior correlates of statement credibility: Theories, paradigms and results. In H Wegener, F. Losel, & J. Haisch (Eds.), Criminal behavior and the justice system: Psychological perspectives (pp. 271-289) New York. Springer-Verlag.

Kraut, R. E. (1978). Verbal and nonverbal cues in the perception of lying. Journal of Personality and Social Psychology 36:380-391.

Kraut R. E. and D. Poe (1980). On the line: The deception judgments of customs inspectors and laymen. Journal of Personality and Social Psychology 36 380-391.

Krebs JR, and R. Dawkins (1984). Animal signals: mind reading and manipulation, in Behavioral Ecology: An Evolutionary, 2nd Edition. Edited by Krebs JR, Davies NB. Sutherland, MA, Sinauer, 1984, pp 380-402

Leslie, L. Z. (1992, Spring). Lying in prime time: Ethical egoism in situation comedies. Journal of Mass Media Ethics, pp. 5-18.

Lockard JS, Kirkevold BC, Kaulk DF: Cost-benefit indexes of deception in nonviolent crime. Bulletin of the Psychonomic Society 16:303-306, 1980

Loftus E. F. (1975). Leading Questions and the Eyewitness Report. Cognitive Psychology 7:560-572.

Loftus E. F. and G. Zanni (1975). Eyewitness Testimony: The influence of the wording of a question. Bulletin of the Psychonomic Society, 5:86-88.

Lykken, D.T. (1981). A Tremor in the Blood: Uses and abuses of the Lie Detector. New York. McGraw Hill.

Lykken, D.T. (1974). Psychology and the Lie Detection Industry. American Psychologist 29, 725-739).

Lykken, D.T. (1960). The Validity of the Guilty Knowledge Technique: The effects of faking. Journal of Applied Psychology 44, 258-262.

MacHovec, Frank J., (1989) Interview And Interrogation, a scientific approach. Charles C. Thomas Publisher, Springfield, IL.

Manning, Peter Kirby 1977. Police work: The organization of policing. Cambridge Mass: MIT Press.

Miller, Walter (1958). Lower Class Culture as a Generating Milieu of Gang Delinquency. Journal of Social Issues 14 (3):5-19.

Nirenberg, Gerard I.: The Art of Negotiating. New York, Cornerstone Library, 1968.

Nirenberg, Jesse S.: Getting Through to People. Englewood Cliffs, Prentice-Hall, 1963.

O'Connor, Joseph and John Seymour (1993). Introducing Neuro-Linguistic Programming: Psychological Skills for Understanding and Influencing People. Aquarian/Thorsons. London.

OSS Assessment Staff: Assessment of Men, Selection of Personnel for the Office of Strategic Services. New York, Rinehart. 1948.

Rabon, Don, Investigative Discourse Analysis (Durham, NC: Carolina Academic Press, 1994), 17.

Raskin DC, Kircher JC (1987). The validity of Lykken's criticisms: fact or fancy? Jurimetrics 27:271-277.

Raskin DC, Podlensky JA (1979). Truth and deception: a reply to Lykken. Psychol Bull 86:54-59, 1979

Raskin DC, Kircher JC, Horowitz SW, (1989). Recent laboratory and field research on polygraph techniques, in Credibility Assessment. Edited by Yuille JC. Dordrecht (Netherlands), Kluwer Academic Publications, 1989 pp 1-24

Raskin, David C. and John C. Kircher (1988). Human Versus Computerized Evaluations of Polygraph Data in a Laboratory Setting Journal of Applied Psychology. Vol. 73 No. 2 pp 291-302. American Psychological Association. Inc.

Riggio R. E. and H. S. Friedman (1983). Individual Differences and ues to deception. Journal of Personality and Social Psychology 45, 899-915.

Rosenberg, Morris and Turner, Ralph H. Social Psychology (1981). Basic Books Inc. New York, NY.

Sapir, Avinoam (1987). Scientific Content Analysis Basic Training Manual. Phoenix, AZ.

Sapir, Avinoam (1998). Scientific Content Analysis Basic HQ Training Seminar. Phoenix, AZ.

Sapir, Avinoam (2000). LSI Scientific Content Analysis. World Wide Web. WWW.LSISCAN.COM.

Saxe, L. (1991, April). Lying. American Psychologist, pp. 409-415.

Schafer, John R. (2008) "Text Bridges and the Micro-Action Interview" FBI Law Enforcement Bulletin January 2008 Volume 77 Number 1

Solomon, R. C. (1993). What a tangled web: deception and self-deception in philosophy, in Lying and Deception in Everyday Life. Edited by Lewis M, Saarni C. New York, Guilford, 1993 pp 30-58

Staff Writer (July 1999). "Liar, Liar, Face on Fire." Discover. Vol.20 No.7 R & D

Stewart, Charles J., and Cash, William B.: Interviewing. Dubuque, William C. Brown, 1978.

Stiff J. B., Miller G. R. (1986). "Come to think of it...": interrogative probes, deceptive communication, and deception detection. Human Communication Research 12:339-357.

Sykes, GreshamM., and David Matza. "Tehcniques of neutralization: A Theory of Delinquency," American Sociological Review 22 (December 1957), 664-670.

Taylor SE, and J.D. Brown (1998). Illusion and well-being: a social psychological perspective on mental health. Psychol Bull 103:193-210, 1988

Tulving, Endel. (1983). Elements of Episodic Memory. New York, NY: Oxford University Press.

Van Damme, Guy I.M.L. (1998). The Trusterpro Reliability Test. Westbrook, South - Africa.

Vrij Aldert and Gun R. Semin (Spring 1996). "Lie Experts' Beliefs About Nonverbal Indicators of Deception." Journal of Nonverbal Behavior Vol. 20, #1.

Vrij, Aldert (1991). "Misverstanden tueesn politie en allochtonen: sociaal-psychologische aspecten van verdacht zijn. Amstersam VU Uitgeverij.

Vrij, A., J. H. Foppes, D. M. Volger, and F. W. Winkel (1992). Moeilijk te bepalen wie de waarheid spreekt: nonverbal gedrag belangrijkste indicator. Algemeen Politie Blad, 141, 13-15

Vrij, A. and F. W. Winkel (1992); Cross-culture police-citizen interactions: The influence of race, beliefs, and nonverbal communication on impression formation. Journal of Applied Social Psychology, 22, 1546-1559.

Walters Stan B. (1996). Principles of Kinesics Interview and Interrogation CRC Press, New York.

Wicks, Robert J., and Josephs, Ernest H., Jr.: Techniques in Interviewing for Law Enforcement and Corrections Personnel. Springfield, Charles C Thomas, 1972.

Wile I: Lying as a biological and social phenomenon. Nervous Child 1:293-313, 1942

Wimmer, H.; S. Gruber, and J. Perner: Young children's conception of lying: moral intuition and denotation and connotation of 'to lie'. Developmental Psychology 21(6):993-995, 1985

Wise, David (1973). The Politics of Lying: Government Deception, Secrecy, and Power. Random House. Inc. New York.

Witkin G: The hunt for a better lie detector: new technology probes the criminal mind. U.S. News and World Report 114(18):49, 1993

Wolfgang, Marvin E. ( 1958). Patterns in Criminal Homicide. Philadelphia: University of Pennsylvania Press.

Woody, Robert H., and Woody, Jane D. (Eds.): Clinical Assessment in Counseling and Psychotherapy. New York, Appleton, Century, Crofts, 1972.

Wright, Karen. (July, 2001). "Go Ahead, Try to Lie." Discover Vol. 22. No. 7. Page 21.

Yeschke, Charles (1993). Interviewing: A Forensics Guide To Interrogation 2nd ed Charles C. Thomas Publisher, Springfield Ill

Yeschke Charles L. (1997). The Art of Investigative Interviewing: A Human Approach to Testimonial Evidence. - Butterworth-Heinemann 1997    Abbr. in text as :  AII (Yeschke,1997)

Zuckerman M, and R. E. Driver R E: (1985) Telling lies: Verbal and nonverbal correlates of deception. In A. W. Siegman, and S. Feldstein (Eds). Mulitchannel Integrations of Nonverbal Behavior pp. 129-147 Hillsdale NJ. Erlbaum.

Zuckerman M, B. M. DePaulo, and R. Rosenthal (1981). Verbal and Nonverbal communication of deception. In L. Berkowitz (Ed.). Advances in experimental social psychology, Vol 14 (pp1-59) New York. Academic Press.

# Detailed Outline

**Deception Management Title Page**
**Section 1: FOUNDATIONS** ........................................................... 1
    WARNING ........................................................................................ 1
    What is Deception Management? ................................................. 1
**Chapter 1 DECEPTION BASICS** ........................................... 5
    Introduction and Definitions ......................................................... 5
    Reasons for Deception .................................................................. 7
    Methods of Deception ................................................................... 7
        Content Editing ....................................................................... 8
        Question Avoidance and Redirection .................................. 9
        Response Falsification ......................................................... 10
**Chapter 2 STUDYING DECEPTION** ..................................... 13
**Chapter 3 BEHAVIORAL GUIDEBOOK** ............................. 17
    Why Deception Indicators Exist: ............................................... 18
    Rules of Behavior ........................................................................ 18
    Rules of Deceptive Behavior ..................................................... 20
    Baselines ........................................................................................ 22
**Section 2: Deception Identification** ......................................... 25
**Chapter 4 UNCONSCIOUS BEHAVIORS** ........................... 29
    Autonomic Nervous System ...................................................... 29
**Chapter 5: SUBCONSCIOUS BEHAVIORS** ......................... 35
    Kinesics and Body Language .................................................... 36
    How Body Language Indicates Deception: ............................. 36
    Actions Involving the Entire Body ........................................... 40
    Face ................................................................................................ 41
    Limbs Hands and Feet ................................................................ 46
        Non Gesture Actions ............................................................ 46
        Gestures ................................................................................. 48
    Vocal Indicators .......................................................................... 51
    Internal Dialogue ......................................................................... 54
    Graphology (Handwriting) Analysis ........................................ 56
**Chapter 6 CONSCIOUS BEHAVIORS** ................................. 59
    Controlling Behaviors ................................................................ 60
    Intimidation .................................................................................. 60
        Name Dropping .................................................................... 60

| | |
|---|---|
| Faked Anger | 61 |
| Kinesic Control | 61 |
| Interview Hijacking | 62 |
| Excessive Attentiveness | 62 |
| Response Manipulation | 63 |
|     Stalling | 63 |
|     Qualified Response | 64 |
|     Response Avoidance | 65 |
|     Rambling | 66 |
| Excuses | 67 |
| Denials | 68 |
| Objections | 69 |
| Conclusions and Summary | 71 |
| **Chapter 7 EXPRESSION ANALYSIS** | **73** |
| Using Expressions in Analysis | 73 |
| Identification of Deceptive Expressions | 74 |
|     Repressed Expressions | 74 |
|     Micro Expressions | 74 |
|     Subtle Expressions | 75 |
|     Asymmetrical Expressions | 75 |
|     Expression Masking (False Expressions) | 76 |
|     Multimodal Comparisons | 77 |
| Emotions and Their Expressions | 77 |
|     Fear | 78 |
|     Anger | 79 |
|     Contempt | 79 |
|     Surprise | 80 |
|     Disgust | 80 |
|     Sadness | 81 |
|     Happiness (Smile) | 81 |
| Summary and Conclusion | 83 |
| **Chapter 8 DISCOURSE ANALYSIS** | **85** |
| Introduction | 85 |
| Component Analysis | 89 |
|     Event Statement Balance | 89 |
|     Content Use of Time and Space | 93 |
|     Unexpected, Inappropriate and Absent Information | 93 |
|     Things Not Done | 97 |

| | |
|---|---|
| Names and Titles | 97 |
| Nouns | 98 |
| Pronouns | 99 |
| Verbs | 100 |
| Summary/Conclusion | 100 |
| **Chapter 9 COMPARATIVE ANALYSIS** | **101** |
| Deception Identification Summary | 104 |
| Motivation and Decision | 104 |
| Construction | 104 |
| Communication Process | 104 |
| The Product | 105 |
| Conclusion | 105 |
| **Section 3: Obtaining Information** | **106** |
| **Chapter 10 INTERVIEWING** | **107** |
| Rules and Guidelines of Interviewing | 107 |
| Interview Preparations | 108 |
| Preparing the Interviewer Emotionally | 108 |
| Environmental Preparations (Setting the Stage) | 108 |
| **Chapter 11 ANTI-DECEPTION INTERVIEWING** | **113** |
| Requesting Assistance | 113 |
| Questioning | 114 |
| Rules of Questioning | 114 |
| Question Form | 118 |
| Question Function | 120 |
| **Chapter 12 TAKING NOTES** | **125** |
| Introduction | 125 |
| Physical Arrangements | 125 |
| The Notepad | 126 |
| Managing the Notepad | 127 |
| Taking Notes | 127 |
| Note Taking Guide (Note Taking Solutions) | 128 |
| Note Taking Tips | 133 |
| **Chapter 13 CONTROL** | **135** |
| Concluding the Interview | 137 |
| Analysis Procedure(s) | 137 |
| **Chapter 14 ELICITING HONESTY** | **139** |
| Introduction | 139 |
| Fear Management | 139 |

| | |
|---|---|
| Two Components for Eliciting Honesty | 140 |
|     Recognizing Deception Prone Situations | 140 |
|     Discouraging Deception as an Option | 142 |
|     Fear Management | 143 |
|     Rapport | 143 |
|     Persuasion | 144 |
|     Additional Rapport Information | 147 |
|     Presentation of Self | 147 |
| **Chapter 15 RESPONDING TO DECEPTION** | 151 |
| Identified Topics of Concern | 152 |
| Investigate External Information | 152 |
| Verifying Information | 153 |
| **Chapter 16: OVERCOMING RESISTANCE** | 155 |
| Introduction | 155 |
| Fear Displacement Introductions | 156 |
|     Procedure | 157 |
|     Fear Reduction (Reducing Concern) | 157 |
|     Overcoming Fears | 158 |
|     Normalization of Behavior | 159 |
|     Exaggerated Comparisons | 160 |
| **Chapter 17 THE DECEPTION MANAGEMENT DIFFERENCE** | 165 |
| Final Considerations | 165 |
| Concluding Thoughts | 166 |
| **Referenced Materials** | 167 |

Made in the USA
Las Vegas, NV
18 June 2021